Fetzer Vineyards, Hopland

Helen Wike

Mendocino County's Wineries & Breweries

Leggett

Covelo

1

101

162

Laytonville

Westport

Pacific Star Winery

North Coast Brewing Company

Fort Bragg

"Skunk Train"

Willits

Caspar

20

Potter Valley

Frey Vineyards
Gabrielli Winery

Redwood Valley Cellar
(Barra & Braren Paul
Fife "Redwood" Vineyards

Fetzer Tasting Room

Mendocino

Lolonis Winery

Little River

Redwood Valley

Albion

20

128

Parducci Wine Estate

Dunnewood Vineyards

Christine Woods Vineyards
Claudia Springs Winery
Handley Cellars
Pepperwood Springs Vineyards
Roederer Estate
Lazy Creek Vineyards
Greenwood Ridge Vineyards
Navarro Vineyards
Pacific Echo Cellars

Navarro

Elk

Ukiah Brewing Company

Ukiah

Germain-Robin

Brutocao Cellars
Domaine Saint Gregory
Hidden Cellars
Elizabeth Vineyards
Mendocino Hill Winery
Mendocino Brewing Company

Zellerbach Winery

Lonetree Winery

Whaler Vineyards

Husk Vineyards
Edmeades Estate
Brutocao Cellars

Philo

Jepson Vineyards

253

Boonville

Anderson Valley Brewing Company

Manchester

Hopland

Duncan Peak Vineyards

Fetzer/Bonterra Vineyards
McDowell Valley Vineyards

175

Milone Family Winery

Point Arena

128

Martz Vineyards

Yorkville Vineyards

101

Yorkville

1

Anchor Bay
Gualala

Cloverdale

Mendocino County

*Recipes from Wineries, Breweries,
Restaurants, Inns and Culinary Resources
of Mendocino County, California*

Compiled and Edited
by
Gail & Bruce Levene

Pacific Transcriptions
Mendocino, California

Library of Congress Catalog Number: 86-60038
ISBN Number: 0-933391-18-8

Manufactured in the United States of America

The recipes in this book have been received directly from the contributors and printed with their permission. A few recipes were previously printed in the first edition of this book. The following recipes are copyrighted by their creators:
Sautéed Sea Vegetables with Honey, Carrot and Rice and *Roasted Nori and Vegetables Fried Rice* are reprinted by permission from *Sea Vegetable Gourmet Cookbook and Wildcrafter's Guide* ©1996 by Eleanor and John Lewallen; *Cheese-And-Wine Bread* is reprinted from *Cafe Beaujolais* ©1984 by Margaret Fox; *Circle T Chicken* is reprinted from the *Ale & Hearty Cookbook.*
Specific copyrights apply to the the following recipes by John Ash: *Cous Cous Risotto with Wild Mushrooms, Pecorino Cheese and Smoked Tomato Jus* © 1996, Revised 8/98; *Wild Mushroom Salad with a Corn Mustard Dressing* ©2000; *Tomatillo, Poblano and Heirloom Bean Chowder* ©1996, Revised 3/2000.

Thanks to Judy Tarbell, Black Bear Press, and Chris Calder for their help.

Contents

Elizabeth Vineyards & Mendocino Hill Winery Tasting Room, Hopland

Wines, Beer & Cooking

This book contains 122 recipes from the wineries, breweries, restaurants, inns and culinary providers of Mendocino County. Its goal is to provide a taste of the choice food products available in California's most beautiful area. As the recipes adequately describe cooking, this brief introduction concerns wine, and its usage with food, followed by facts regarding the County's breweries plus information about the Farmers Market.

In 1966, 5,617 acres of vineyards were planted with grapes in Mendocino County, and the only bonded winery was Parducci, founded in Ukiah in 1932. By 1974 there were 8,727 acres of vineyards and 7 wineries.

Today, Mendocino County has 13,000 acres of grapes in cultivation, 300 vineyards, and a wider range (8) of vineyard microclimates— wine-growing regions or "appelations"— than any other California county. The region is a leader in organic viticulture and 25% of its vineyard acreage is organically farmed. 37 wineries produce more than 80 different kinds of award-winning wines.

Mendocino County falls within the same degree of latitude as the famous vineyards of France, Italy and Germany, but it has been blessed with a more stable climate than Europe's premium wine growing regions. In northern California grapes grow during long warm dry summers, with fog in the morning and cool ocean breezes at night. This enables winemakers to use grapes that have distinctive characteristics.

In fact, Mendocino County produces wines of extraordinary quality, which have won a disproportionate share of awards for their excellence in competitions. This is remarkable, considering the relative youth of most wineries. But because the County's growers take such pride in their grapes, the wineries now make the finest California's wines, and some may well be the best in the world.

There is a great mystique about wine and confusion about its use, particularly with food. We have all heard "don't drink white wine with red meat" and that "wine is a living thing" or seen a waiter handle a bottle of wine like it was new-born baby. To examine in depth these peculiarities is a task beyond this book. What we can do is pass along some of our experiences with wine and food, that hopefully will enhance your own drinking and eating pleasures.

You should achieve a balance. Wine, remember, is a food, to be drunk for enjoyment, not something for show or prestige. Nor should wine be an intimidating purchase. You want a good wine to enhance a good meal and vice versa—learning to pair the two is the goal. You have to use your imagination and/or memory to think how a specific wine will taste with a particular food. It is not necessarily an easy task, but really just experience, of testing tastes and trusting your palate to find what YOU enjoy most—not what a wine expert says you should drink. In fact, no one else can say what tastes best to you.

This is how the reknowned wine writer, Hugh Johnson, put it:

"Good wine, red or white, sweet or dry, has a distinct, clean, consistent, and harmonious character all the way from first sip to last swallow. Better wine, quite simply, has more of the same. And the best has most: of scents, flavors, and, perhaps most of all, of lingering aromas that hang about palate and throat long after you have swallowed."

Grapes have four usages: 1. fresh at table, 2. raisins, 3. sweet juice, 4. wine.

Wine is divided into four main categories (a fifth is wine made from fruits other than grapes):

1. Appetizer wines, usually made with intentionally oxidized flavors, e.g. Vermouth, which is herbalized and fortified.

2. Dessert wines, which are still, natural and very sweet.

3. Sparkling wines, which are natural and carbonated at least 7 pounds per square inch.

4. Table wines, which are still, natural and fermented from fresh ripe grapes.

Wines in each of these categories are made in Mendocino County, plus some world-class alambic brandies.

Sparkling Wines come in many styles and colors, accompany all kinds of foods and go well with appetizers, entrees and desserts. The premier type, of course, is champagne, which in the U.S. is a generic word for white or pink sparkling wine. By law a champagne label must state the method by which it is produced, one of three: a."Methode Champenoise," or "fermented in the bottle," the classical method, using hand labor, made from quality grape varieties and usually the highest priced; b. "Bottle fermented" or "Transfer process," using machines that remove the wine from its original bottle, then replace it; c. "Charmat process" or "Bulk process," when the wine is fermented in large tanks, then bottled.

Champagne is also noted on the label by a rather indefinite degree of sweetness: 1. Natural—very dry, no sweetness 2. Brut—dry, little or no sweetness 3. Extra Dry—light or faintly sweet 4. Sec—quite sweet 5. Demi Sec—very sweet. With champagne, even more than with still table wines, experiment to find what suits your taste.

Table Wine describes a whole class of naturally fermented wines, used as mealtime accompaniments to food. Most are "dry", with only a little or no sugar remaining. Some are sweet, really more appropriate as dessert wines—they retain their classification as table wines because percentage of alcohol, not sweetness, is the tax base for wines. Labels usually state this percentage. Some labels also contain statistical information about residual sugars and other data.

Table wines are divided into three sub-groups:

1. Generic Wines, usually blends of several different grape varieties, are often named after a European wine area such as Burgundy, Chablis or the Rhine, or simply called Mountain Red, Vin Rose, or White Table Wine. These wines are inexpensive and may be quite good, but the kinds of grapes or the locales where grown aren't normally indicated.

2. Varietal Wines are made from and named after a single grape variety. A "vintage dated varietal" (the year it was bottled appears on the label) must contain 75% of the wine grape on the label, and 95% of the wine in that bottle must be from grapes crushed at the date specified.

3. Proprietary Wines are usually blends, labeled with special names (that may or may not have a particular meaning) invented by a specific winery. The varietal wines will usually be listed on the label.

White, Red, and Rose´ wines are distinctly different kinds of wines, but wine grapes are usually black or white, not red. At its beginning all wine is white. By allowing the skins to remain in the vat long enough after crushing, various tints of pink or red are produced. By leaving the stems in the vat, which add tannin, another characteristic is achieved. These timings are winemaking skills.

Tasting Wine—The University of California at Davis has developed a point scoring system consisting of 10 elements to be judged in wine tasting. It's fun to use, but probably all you care about is if the wine is pleasing to drink; so the descriptions can be cut down to four: sight, smell, taste and texture.

Cooking with Wine—Regard wine as another flavoring agent in your cooking, a condiment to add a new dimension to your foods. A few things to keep in mind: 1. During cooking, the alcohol in wine evaporates—what's left are flavorful (and calorie-free) wine residues. 2. Use only a small amount of wine when cooking, so wine flavors blend subtly with the foods. Otherwise food tastes will be overpowered by the wine. 3. Using wine as a marinade will tenderize meat and bring out the flavors. **Do Not** marinate in metal, as this may interact with the wine. Use porcelain or glass. 4. You can substitute wine for any liquid used in a recipe, as long as the wine chosen is compatible with the other ingredients. Examples are: fish poached in white wine and water; red wine used with tomato sauces, white wine added to cream sauces; a portion of light white wine (e.g. Muscat or Viognier) substituted for water in a cake recipe. 5. Always serve the same or a similar wine like that used in cooking your food. Otherwise there may be taste conflicts.

Brutocao Cellars, Hopland

Wine & Food—Now usually a safe guideline is that red wine goes best with beef and lamb, red or white wine with poultry, white wine with fish and seafood. But this doesn't always hold true. It's possible, for example, to enjoy chopped sirloin with White Riesling, if the circumstances call for it (which recently they did for us, because that's what was available). And a strong fish like salmon just might mask the taste of a light white wine.

To repeat, experiment and discover what suits your own palate. Here are some cautionary suggestions, given as recommendations only—you may not agree!

Wine & Eggs—Both in cooking and serving one should be careful with the wine used. Red wines are almost never appropriate. If you must have wine with eggs, use a light white.

Wine & Salads—Salads and wine go extremely well together, but salad dressings and wine are totally incompatible. Virtually all salad dressings contain acids, which will make wine taste terrible. Unless you eat salads without dressing (as I do), you should forego wine until after the salad course. A Crab Louie is a problem. If wine is necessary with a salad and dressing, make it a very light white.

Wine & Cheese—Although the usage is firmly fixed in memory, and you've seen artistic photographs in numerous books and magazines, there is a great dispute in the wine and food world about serving wine with cheese. Some experts maintain that wine and cheese are perfectly complementary; others disagree, feeling that cheese overpowers wine, except for the strongest reds. Some believe a light cheese, like Gouda or Mozzarella, would be inappropriate with a heavy red, but would go quite well with, say, a Sauvignon Blanc. You have to make your own personal choices.

Wine & Coffee—A wine expert has observed that "pairing wine and coffee is like inviting an estranged couple to dinner." Said another way, if you want to destroy the warm feeling that comes after a good meal with a good wine, drink a cup of coffee. Coffee's oily bitterness, particularly coffee roasted directly over propane gas burners by self-proclaimed gourmet coffee companies, will make you forget you even drank any wine. And ingesting hyrocarbons absorbed by coffee oils is certainly detrimental to your health!

Learning to pair wine and food is a skill—learning about wine itself is an art. Hundreds of books, numerous magazines, even on-line courses, are available to the curious—and curiosity is essential, considering that more than 80 different kinds of wine are produced by the County's wineries.

In Mendocino County, the Mendocino Winegrowers Alliance, a non-profit organization of grapegrowers and winemakers, promotes our winegrowing industry. The Alliance is involved in tastings and seminars, educational and promotional functions, and other activities aimed at continually improving the quality and reputation of Mendocino grapes and wine.

Mendocino County Micro-Craft Breweries

Almost every small town in Mendocino County once had a brewery that made local beer. But the rise of the Temperance Movement over a hundred years ago and local control gradually forced most breweries out of business—passage of the 18th Amendment in 1919 closed those that remained.

Beer would not be produced again commercially in Mendocino County until 1983, when the Hopland Brewery became the first Brewpub in California since before Prohibition. The brewery sold out its first bottlings and each month in 1984 set new sales records. Through the years the Mendocino Brewing Company has continued to expand production.

Today the company has five labels—Red Tail Ale, Blue Heron Pale Ale, Peregrine Pale Ale, Black Hawk Stout and Eye of the Hawk— plus two seasonal products: Yuletide Porter and Springtide Ale.

Mendocino Brewing Company has received numerous awards for both its beers and their packaging. In1997, the company won four awards in the World Beer Championship, with Red Tail Ale receiving a Gold Medal. Red Tail Ale was also proclaimed a Top Ten Beer of 1996 (including European brews) by Wine Enthusiast magazine. The Underground Wine Journal also awarded Blue Heron Pale Ale a Gold Medal and Red Tail Ale received another Gold Medal from the World Beer Championship in 1999.

In 1999 Mendocino Brewery Company celebrated its 16th Anniversary as a pioneer and playing a major role in changing the taste of the beer world. To thank local communities for their support, the company staged the Red Tail Ale Americana Music Festival, a fund-raiser/celebration for various non-profit organizations in Mendocino and Sonoma Counties.

From a modest 10-barrel beginning in 1987, beneath the Buck Horn Saloon in Boonville, the Anderson Valley Brewing Company has steadily expanded its production and its new state-of-the-art brew house on a 30-acre site at the eastern end of Boonville is capable of producing 60,000 barrels a year.

Anderson Valley Brewing Company bottles Boont Amber Ale, Barney Flats Oatmeal Stout, Hop Ottin' India Pale Ale, Poleeko Gold Pale Ale and Belk's ESB Extra Special Bitter Ale plus several other special brews: St. David's Belgian Ale, Red Belgian Ale, Millennium Ale, and Raspberry Wheat Beer, the latter made with only fresh, locally grown, organic raspberries. Using fruit from its own organic raspberry garden makes AVBC the first estate brewery in California.

Anderson Valley Brewing Company was twice listed as one of the Top Ten Breweries of the Year (1996 & 1997) at the World Beer Championships.

The North Coast Brewing Company occupies a new facility in Fort Bragg with an annual brewing capacity of 22,000 barrels. The company also owns a 75 seat restaurant, a full kitchen, a bar licensed to sell beer and wine, and an additional 1200 barrel brewery.

Since 1988 the brewery has bottled Ruedrich's Red Seal Ale, Scrimshaw Pilsner Beer, Old No. 38 Stout, Blue Star Wheat Beer, Old Rasputin Russian Imperial Stout, Pranqster and the Acme label, plus seasonal offerings like Oktoberfest Ale and Traditional Bock. Of historical interest is Acme California Pale Ale, which traces its heritage back to 1861 in San Francisco

In 1992, NCBC was awarded four medals (one gold, two silver and a bronze) at the Great American Beer Festival in Denver. In 1998, the brewery was named as one of the "10 Best Breweries in the World" by Chicago's Beverage Testing Institute at the World Beer Championships.

Old Rasputin Imperial Stout (another brew of historical note) won gold medals in Chicago in 1998 and in Chicago and Vail, Colorado in 1996.

Mendocino County's newest micro-craft brewery—Ukiah Brewing Company & Restaurant—opened in Spring, 2000 in an historic building in downtown Ukiah. The company plans to use as many certified organic products as possible in its state-of-the art brewery and restaurant. The first batch of beer produced—OPA Organic Pale Ale—as of this writing available only on tap—has been well received by beer aficiandos.

Mendocino County Farmers Market, Mendocino

Mendocino County Farmers Markets

Between early May and the end of October, Farmers Markets take place every week at seven locations throughout Mendocino County. They are one of the culinary joys that locals and visitors alike may enjoy.

"Certified Farmers' markets are places where genuine farmers sell their crops directly to the public, The certified producer certificate posted at each sellers space is the customer's guarantee of buying directly from the grower, his family or employee. Before a farmer can sell at a Certified Farmers' Market, the county agricultural commissioner checks to make sure that each seller is growing the commodity he or she sells."

"Our venture is your adventure: Fresh vine and tree ripened fruits and vegetables, often picked the same day. Availability of produce in bulk for preserving. An alternative shopping experience that restores the traditional link between farm and city. Direct communication with farmers. Ask us your questions. Some farmers offer organically grown produce. In season, you will find unique, uncommon and specialized produce. Try our gourmet, connoisseur, new and heirloom varieties plus Asian fruits and vegetables."

BOONVILLE
      —Boonville Hotel Parking Lot—Saturday 10 -12:00
FORT BRAGG
      —Laurel & Franklin Streets—Wednesday 3:30 - 6:00
GUALALA
      —Gualala Community Center—Saturday 3:00 - 5:00
LAYTONVILLE
      —Good Food Store Highway 101—Sunday 2:30 - 5:00
MENDOCINO
      —Howard Street South—Friday 12:00 - 2:00
UKIAH
      —Orchard Plaza Shopping Center—Saturday 8:30 - 12:00
      —School & Clay Streets—Tuesday 3:00 - 6:00
WILLITS
      —City Park—Thursday 3:00 - 6:00pm

Information from:
Mendocino County Farmers Market Association
P.O. Box 2176, Fort Bragg, CA 95437
      —Boonville: 895-9477—Fort Bragg: 937-4330 or 964-0536
      —Gualala: 882-2474—Laytonville: 984-8148—Mendocino: 937-2728
      —Ukiah: 743-1342—Willits: 459-5470

Mendocino Brewing Company, Hopland

Appetizers,
Condiments,
&
Sauces

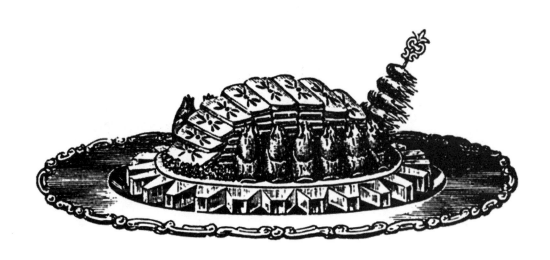

Fife "Redhead" Vineyards, Redwood Valley

Fife "Redhead" Vineyards of Redwood Valley

Karen MacNeil-Fife's
Eat-With-Your-Fingers Spicy Grilled Shrimp

Who says zinfandel must be served with meat? We love zin with all sorts of spicy and grilled dishes including this outrageous (but simple) shrimp dish. To make the shrimp plumper and more juicy, I brine them first. This is very easy to do and the results are remarkable. Also, because the shrimp are grilled in their shells, they stay very moist.

Serves 4 as an appetizer.

> 1 cup Kosher salt
> 1 pound frozen jumbo or very large shrimp, shell on
> 1/2 cup olive oil
> 1 teaspoon paprika
> 1 teaspoon tumeric
> 1 teaspoon ground cumin
> 1 teaspoon cracked black pepper
> 1/2 teaspoon salt
> 1 teaspoon Tandoori paste*
> 1 tablespoon minced garlic

To brine the shrimp, pour 1 cup of boiling water into a large bowl. Add the salt and stir until salt is dissolved. Stir in 1 1/2 quarts of cold water. Add the frozen shrimp (do not peel). Place bowl in refrigerator for 1 to 1 1/2 hours. Drain shrimp and rinse with cold running water. Spread on a paper towel and pat dry. Shrimp is now ready to use.

Prepare marinade by mixing all remaining ingredients together in a bowl. Add shrimp, tossing to coat. Cover bowl with plastic wrap and refrigerate for at least 1 hour.

Lightly brush a clean grill with vegetable oil. Heat to medium-high. Throw shrimp on the grill. Using tongs, turn each shrimp when the side exposed to the heat turns a bright red and takes on grill marks (usually about 3 to 5 minutes). Cook briefly on second side. Shrimp is completely done when the shell begins to split open down the back.

Heap shrimp on a platter and serve family style with plenty of napkins—*and* Fife Redhead Zinfandel.

*Tandoori paste is available in better supermarkets and most specialty shops. Patak's is a very good brand.

19

Mendocino Mustard of Fort Bragg

Seeds & Suds Shrimp Pate

1/4 pound bay shrimp, cooked
6 small cloves garlic
2 tablespoons Seeds & Suds Mendocino Mustard
2 tablespoons fresh lemon juice
2 tablespoons sweet butter at room temperature
1 tablespoon whipping cream
1 tablespoon dry sherry
1 teaspoon fresh dill, chopped
salt and pepper, to taste

Blend all ingredients in food processor until smooth. Chil until ready to serve. Garnish with fresh dill.

Serve with crackers or cucumber slices.

Serves 8-10 as an appetizer.

Handley Cellars of Philo

Cucumber Wasabi Canapés

1 cucumber *(Japanese cucumbers are best if you can find them)*
3-4 ounces cream cheese, brought to room temperature
1 teaspoon prepared wasabi (Japanese horseradish)
lemon zest *(lemon zesters are handy little tools found in cookware
     stores; they remove the lemon zest, but not the bitter white pith)*
finely chopped chives

Place cream cheese in a bowl and whip it with a fork until light and fluffy. Add wasabi and re-mix.

Using vegetable peeler, peel cucumber, leaving very thin strips of peel to create a pleasing striped effect. Slice into rounds. Spread cream cheese thinly atop cucumber slices and garnish with lemon zest and chives.

Serve with Handley Sauvignon Blanc.

McDowell Valley Vineyards of Hopland

Crab Mold With Goat Cheese & Lemon Thyme

1 tablespoons unflavored gelatin in 2 tablespoons water

3 tablespoons fresh lemon juice

2 teaspoons lemon zest, minced

1 cup fresh-picked crab, chopped

1 tablespoon green onion, minced

1 8 ounce can cream of onion soup

5 ounces fresh goat cheese

3 ounces fresh cream cheese

1 teaspoon Dijon style mustard

2 tablespoons fresh lemon thyme

1 cup mayonnaise

Spray a 4 cup, decorative mold with a non-stick spray.

Dissolve gelatin in water.

Remove zest from lemon and mince; squeeze juice.

Clean crab if necessary and chop; mince green onions and herbs. *(Lobster bisque soup and lobster can be substituted for the cream of onion soup and fresh crab).*

Crumble goat and cream cheeses into the soup; add mustard and gelatin and cook for 5 minutes, stirring constantly with a whisk. Add minced onion, herbs, lemon juice, zest and mayonnaise, blend together; fold in crab.

Pour into mold (mixture should be no more than 2-3 inches deep) and refrigerate until set.

Unmold onto serving plate, garnish, and return to refrigerator for 30 minutes before serving.

Serve with unsalted crackers or thin slices of rye, French or pumpernickel bread.

Makes 4 cups of crab mixture

The perfect complement for McDowell Viognier, Marsanne and Grenache Rosé.

Joshua Grindle Inn of Mendocino

Arlene's
Spicy Crab And Goat Cheese Puffs

Shells:

1/2 package frozen puff pastry (one sheet)

Filling:

4 ounces fresh crab meat

3 ounces soft goat cheese at room temperature

1/4 cup mayonnaise

1 tablespoon chopped green onion

1 teaspoon lemon juice

dash of Tabasco

salt and pepper to taste

parsley sprigs

Thaw pastry at room temperature for 30 minutes. Unfold pastry on lightly floured surface and roll into 12" x 18" rectangle. Cut into 24 three inch squares (four across and six down). Fill two mini-muffin tins with a pastry square in each cup. Press pastry into place with tips of squares extending above muffin cups.

Put all filling ingredients in a medium sized bowl and combine until well mixed. Fill each pastry shell with one teaspoon crab cheese filling. Chill for a minimum of one hour.

Bake at 375° for fifteen minutes and serve immediately.

Garnish with parsley sprigs.

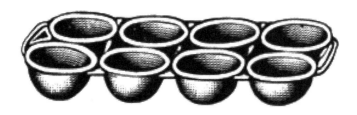

Mendosa's Market of Mendocino

Chuck & Mary Moffett's
Smoked Salmon Pizza

1 packaged puff pastry sheet
8 ounces cream cheese
2 ounces sour cream or plain yogurt
1/2 teaspoon garlic powder
1 teaspoon dill (dried)
1 1/2 cup smoked salmon, flaked
1/4 cup capers
1/4 cup chopped red onion
1 1/2 cup Mozzarella cheese

Roll out pastry to fit jelly roll pan. Prick with fork and bake in 350° oven until golden brown.

Meanwhile, blend cream cheese, yogurt, garlic and dill until creamy and smooth. Spread over pastry.

Sprinkle salmon, capers and onions evenly. Top with cheese.
Broil until cheese bubbles.

Cut and serve with a salad or as an appetizer.

Jepson Vineyards, Ukiah

Jepson Vineyards, Winery & Distillery of Ukiah

Dave Johnson's
Pesto Pizza with Smoked Salmon and Brie

The ingredients for this stunning appetizer are found 'ready-made'. So...only assembly and oven-baking are required. What could be easier?

1 medium or large pizza shell (thin crust)
1 deli carton fresh pesto (1/2 pint or 1 pint)
1-2 packs thin sliced smoked salmon
1 medium round of brie cheese
Sprinkling of dill or minced parsley

Preheat oven to 450°. Slide pizza shell onto pizza pan and apply a moderately thin coat of pesto.

Slice the brie in thin wedges, right through its crust, and arrange to cover the pizza. You'll have little gaps here and there.

Layer on the thin slices of smoked salmon, distributing as evenly as possible over the surface. Sprinkle on a little dill or parsley.

Bake until crust is done and cheese is bubbly and beginning to brown. Allow to cool slightly, then cut crust into appetizer size pieces.

Pairs beautifully with a Blanc de Blanc.

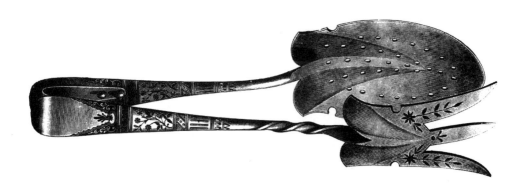

Ukiah Brewing Company & Restaurant of Ukiah

Chef Jennifer Schmitt's
Tofu and Vegetable Skewers
with Spicy Peanut Sauce

Needed:

Skewers
1 pound firm tofu pressed, cut in 1 1/2" cubes
3 Japanese eggplant, cut in 3/4" thick circles
2 red bell peppers, seeded, cut into 1" squares

Marinade:

1 tablespoon ginger, chopped
1 tablespoon garlic, chopped
1/4 cup soy sauce
1/2 cup peanut oil

Peanut Sauce:

1 cup peanut butter
1/2 cup coconut milk
1/2 cup milk or water
2 tablespoon soy sauce
2 cloves finely chopped garlic
1 tablespoon minced ginger
2 fresh Thai chiles or Jalapeno pepper, finely chopped
juice of 1/2 orange
juice of 1 lime
fresh sprigs of Thai basil or cilantro

Make marinade for skewer food. Cut vegetables and tofu as directed and put two of each on an 8" skewer, alternating for color.

Pour marinade into shallow pan and add skewered food. Let sit 2 hours turning occasionally.

26

Make peanut sauce. In a 4 quart sauce pan sauté ginger and garlic in 1 tablespoon peanut oil. Combine peanut butter, coconut milk, water, and soy sauce. Stir on low heat to emulsify. Add chiles for desired heat, then add citrus juices at the end, just before serving.

Grill vegetable skewers on a BBQ or charbroiler until eggplant is soft and tofu is browned.

Serve 2 skewers per plate with 1/4 cup of the peanut sauce on the side in a small bowl.

Brewmeister Bret Cooperrider suggests our pilsener or pale ale to accompany this delicious appetizer.

St. Orres of Gualala

Wild Plum Ketchup

5 pounds plums
4 1/2 cups sugar
2 1/2 cups red wine vinegar
1 teaspoon ground cinnamon
pinch nutmeg
pinch ground clove
2 tablespoons freshly grated ginger
1/2 cup water

In a nonreactive pot, add the plums, sugar, water and ginger. Cover and simmer for about 30 minutes, stirring the mixture frequently to avoid any sticking.

In a separate sauce pan, combine the vinegar and spices and bring to a rigorous boil.

Combine the two mixtures and continue to cook on a medium heat until the mixture has the consistency of a fruit puree. Allow the mixture to cool and pass it through a fine sieve. Bottle and refrigerate.

Harvest Market of Fort Bragg

Hot Mushroom Turnovers

3 3 ounce packages cream cheese, softened
all purpose flour
butter, softened
1/2 pound mushrooms, minced
1 large onion, minced
1 teaspoon salt
1/2 teaspoon thyme leaves
1/4 cup sour cream
1 egg, beaten

In medium bowl at medium speed, mix well cream cheese, 1 1/2 cups flour, and 1/2 cup butter, occasionally scraping bowl. Wrap dough; chill 1 hour.

In 10" skillet over medium heat, cook mushrooms and onion in 3 tablespons butter, until tender.

Stir in salt, thyme leaves and 2 tablespoons flour until blended; stir in sour cream.

On floured surface, thinly roll out half of dough; with cookie cutter, cut twenty 2 3/4" circles. Roll scraps into ball; chill.

On one half of each circle, put a teaspoonfull of mushroom mixture. Brush edges with beaten egg.

Fold dough over filling; with fork, press edges together, prick top, place on ungreased cookie sheets. Repeat with remaining dough and filling.

Brush turnovers with egg. Cover, chill, about 25 minutes. Preheat oven to 450°. Bake turnovers 12 minutes or until golden brown.

Thatcher Inn of Hopland

House Focaccia
with Two Mediterranean Toppings

Focaccia

2 sheet pans (2 round 11 inch pans)
4 cups bread flour
1/2 teaspoon salt
1 3/4 cups warm water
2 1/2 teaspoons dry yeast
3 tablespoons extra virgin olive oil

Mix salt with flour in the mixer bowl. Sprinkle yeast over the warm water. Mix. Let rest until liquid begins to bubble. Pour liquid over flour. Add olive oil.

Using the dough hook, mix 10 minutes on medium speed. Cover with saran wrap. Let rest in a warm place till double in volume. Punch down. Divide in half.

Brush baking sheet with olive oil.

Stretch dough with fingers to cover pan. Place toppings to cover dough. Let rise in warm place for 20 minutes. Bake in preheated oven at 375° until edges brown. Check after 15 minutes.

Toppings: Each Column Is A Different Topping!

Olive Topping	Pimiento Topping
8 ounces calamata olives, chopped	5 ounces pimiento, chopped
3 tablespoons drained capers	3 teaspoons chili pepper flakes
2 tablespoons anchovies, chopped	8 garlic cloves, pressed
1/4 cup olive oil	2 teaspoons ground coriander
2 cloves garlic, pressed	2 teaspoons ground cumin
1 teaspoon black pepper	1 teaspoon salt
1 tablespoon balsamic vinegar	1/4 cup olive oil

Mix all ingredients for each topping. Spread on unbaked dough.

Pacific Echo Cellars, Philo

Pacific Echo Cellars of Philo

Chef Rosemary Campiformio of St. Orres
Yam Pancakes with Sour Cream

1 medium yam, grated
1 Russet potato, grated
2 eggs
4 tablespoons flour
1/8 cup green onion tops, chopped
3 tablespoons heavy cream
1 tablespoon sour cream
2 ounces peanut oil
1 ounce caviar
6 chives, cut in half
salt to taste
red pepper flakes to taste

With the grating attachment of your food processor, grate the yam and the potato.

Combine the grated yam and potato, eggs, flour, green onion and heavy cream in a large mixing bowl. The batter will be loose.

In a large skillet, heat the oil on high and drop approximately two ounces of formed batter. Cook until brown on both sides. Remove the little cakes from the skillet and place them on a clean paper towel.

Repeat with remaining batter.

Allow the cakes to cool slightly.

Fill a pastry bag with the sour cream and pipe a small rosette of sour cream on each pancake.

Divide the caviar equally among the pancakes and place on top of the sour cream.

Garnish with chives and red pepper flakes and serve with Pacific Echo Brut.

The Victorian Farmhouse of Little River

Victorian Crab Caper Sauce Navarro

- **4 teaspoons cornstarch**
- **2/3 cup Navarro Chardonnay Verjus**
- **1 tablespoon butter**
- **1/2 cup chopped green onions**
- **3 tablespoons capers**
- **1/2 cup shredded crab**
- **1 tablespoon dark brown sugar**
- **1/3 cup Navarro Chardonnay Verjus**
- **1/8 cup pine nuts**

1 pound Brie wheel, baked on serving dish
sweet baguette, sliced on diagonal

In skillet, brown butter. Add green onions, lightly sauté. Add capers and crab, mix well, lightly sauté, set aside.

In a small saucepan whisk together cornstarch and 2/3 cup Navarro Chardonnay Verjus. On low heat stir until thickened and clear. Be sure to have no lumps.

Add sauce to caper mixture. Mix well. Add brown sugar, mix well. Add remaining Navarro Chardonnay Verjus to desired consistency. Toss in pine nuts.

This sauce can be made ahead, refrigerated, and reheated. You may need to add more Navarro Chardonnay Verjus to get desired consistency, when you reheat.

Pour hot over baked Brie. Serve with sweet baguette slices, or "sweet" crackers. Can be used over vegetables as well, i.e. asparagus.

Lazy Creek Vineyards of Philo

Hot Artichoke Dip

4 cans water-packed artichoke hearts
2 cups mayonnaise
2 1/2 cups freshly grated quality Parmesan cheese
2 cups chopped canned green chilies

Drain artichoke hearts and coarsely chop (this can be done in a food processor). Add mayonnaise, Parmesan cheese and green chilies.

Spoon into baking dish and bake approximately 20 to 30 minutes in 350° oven or until bubbly and slightly brown on top.

Great with a baguette and a glass of Lazy Creek Chardonnay!

Whaler Vineyard of Ukiah

Whaler Anchovie Hors d' Oeuvres

1 can fillet of anchovies (rolled with capers)
1-2 lemons
1 small onion
crackers (Carr's or Ritz)
crushed ice

Trim lemon peel away from lemon and slice lemon (make thin slices); remove seeds.

Slice onion—again, very thin slices.

Place a slice of lemon on cracker, then place several rings of onion on the lemon. Top with an anchovie rolled with caper (or serve the lemon, onion with anchovies on a bed of crushed ice in a silver bowl with crackers on the side).

Simple and elegant!

Martz Vineyards, Yorkville

Martz Vineyards of Yorkville

Martz's Stuffed Bread
(Not for the faint of heart)

Cut one loaf fresh sourdough bread, lenth-wise. Coat both sides with olive oil, layer with chopped olives, minced fresh garlic, slices of brie and roasted bell peppers.

Place remaining bread on top, wrap in foil and heat until brie melts. Slice and serve hot with a great Cabernet, then take a nap.

Elizabeth Vineyards of Redwood Valley

Anti Pasta

1 cup water
1 cup white vinegar
1 cup celery
1 cup onions
1 cup carrots
1 12 ounce can albacore, drained
1 can sliced olives, drained
1 cup sweet pickles, chopped
14 ounces catsup
3/4 cup oil (less if desired)

Heat water and vinegar and boil celery, onions and carrots until crisp—drain and cool.

Add albacore, olives, pickles, catsup and oil to vegetables. Mix all together and chill at least 4 hours or overnight.

Heritage House of Little River

Remoulade

24 ounces mayonnaise
2 ounces capers, chopped fine
3 tablespoons dill pickles, minced
3 tablespoons chives, minced
3 tablespoons parsley, minced
3 tablespoons tarragon
1 tablespoon Dijon mustard
2 anchovy filets, minced
1/2 teaspoon Worcestershire sauce
1/2 teaspoon Tabasco sauce

Mix all incredients and let chill over night.
Balance with salt and pepper.

Fuller's Fine Herbs of Mendocino

Arlene Fuller's
Mango Green Onion Salsa

1 ripe mango, cut into cubes
1 peach, cubed
1 teaspoon sugar
2 tablespoons minced parsely
2 tablespoons Fuller's Fiesta Herb Vinegar
 green onion, sliced thin
1/4 to 1/2 teaspoon red pepper flakes
juice of 1 lime

Combine all ingredients in a glass bowl and chill for 30 minutes.
Serve this with broiled or poached salmon, ling cod or halibut.

Anderson Valley Brewing Company of Boonville

Caesar Dressing

12 whole garlic cloves (1 ounce)
3 tablespoons AVBC Belk's Extra Special Bitter Mustard
2 1/2 teaspoon anchovy paste
3 tablespoons Worcestershire sauce
5 whole egg yokes

75 milliters AVBC oatmeal stout
50 milliters balsamic vinegar
50 milliters red wine vinegar
350 milliters canola oil

Blend first ingredients well in Cuisinart. Add liquid ingredients and blend well.

Brutocao Cellars of Hopland and Philo

Cranberries Zinfandel

1 bag cranberries
1 cup Brutocao Zinfandel
1 cup sugar
2 tablespoons chopped fresh orange peel
1 stick cinnamon

Boil together wine and sugar. Add remaining ingredients. Cover and simmer about 20 minutes, until berries have burst and sauce has thickened.

Stevenswood Lodge, Little River

Breads
&
Breakfasts

St. Orres Restaurant, Gualala

The Larkin Cottage of Mendocino

Three-Wheat Batter Bread

1 package active dry yeast

1/2 cup warm water

1/8 teaspoon ground ginger

3 tablespoons honey

1 large can (13 ounces) evaporated milk

1 teaspoon salt

2 tablespoons salad oil

2 1/2 cups unsifted flour

1 1/4 cups unsifted whole wheat flour

1/2 cup wheat germ

1/4 cup cracked wheat

In a large bowl, combine yeast, water, ginger and 1 tablespoon of the honey and let stand in a warm place until bubbly (approximately 20 minutes).

Stir in remaining honey, milk, salt and oil.

Mix together remaining ingredients and add to liquid mixture 1 cup at a time, beating until well blended.

Spoon batter evenly into well-greased two-pound coffee can.

Cover the can with well-greased plastic coffee can lid. (You may freeze at this point if you want).

Let rise in a warm place until the lid 'pops off' (about 60-90 minutes).

Bake uncovered in 350° oven for 60 minutes or until bread sounds hollow when tapped.

Let cool on a rack for about 10 minutes, then loosen crust around the edge of the can and then slide the bread from the can and let cool in an upright position on the rack.

Cafe Beaujolais of Mendocino

Margaret Fox's
Cheese-and-Wine Bread

I made up this recipe years ago when I wanted something that showed off both cheese and wine. If you use the large amount of (optional) garlic, you might wish to retitle the recipe 'Cheese-Wine-and-Garlic Bread.'

After a while at the restaurant, you feel as if you've made every kind of sandwich under the sun, so the only thing left is to come up with new bread. We use this one often; it has evolved into a great basis for a large number of recipes. A roast beef sandwich on Cheese-and-Wine Bread is just fantastic. We do it with home-made mayonnaise, mustard, lettuce, tomatoes, and onions. It's delicious with sun-dried tomatoes. We also serve an open-faced vegetable sandwich: tomatoes, lettuce, sprouts if you can stand them, and grated carrots.

6 tablespoons unsalted butter

1 1/2 cups dry white wine

6 tablespoons finely minced garlic (optional)

2 eggs, beaten

1/2 cup minced green onions

1 teaspoon salt

2 packages dry yeast

6 to 6 1/2 cups flour

4 teaspoons sugar

1 pound aged Asiago or dry jack cheese,
    cut into 1/2-inch cubes

1/4 cup warm water

Step 1: Cook onions (and optional garlic)

Sauté onions (and optional garlic) in butter for about 30 seconds, without permitting them to burn. Set aside and cool.

Step 2: Make yeast mixture

Dissolve yeast and sugar in water. Stir and set in warm place for 5 minutes. Mixture should be bubbly. (If it isn't, your yeast may be too old. Check the expiration date on the package, and if it is too old, discard and try again. Better still, check the date before you start.) Stir again.

Step 3: Make dough

In a large bowl, whisk together wine, eggs, salt, and yeast mixture. Gradually add 3 cups flour, and beat for about 3 minutes until elastic threads start to form around edge of bowl. Add cooled garlic and onion mixture, and with a large sturdy wood spoon, beat in 2 1/2 to 3 cups more flour.

Turn dough out on a very lightly floured board, and knead until smooth and springy. (It's OK if it's slightly tacky.) Cover with a clean dry dish towel and let rest 5 minutes. Knead again. Dough should not be tacky at this point; if it is, add 1/4 cup flour and knead 5 more minutes. (You should always knead for 5 minutes after adding flour.)

Step 4: Let dough rise

Place dough in a large greased bowl, turn so it's greased all over, and seal airtight with plastic wrap. Put in a warm place and let rise until doubled—about 1 hour. Punch down, turn out, and knead a few times to pop air bubbles.

Step 5: Add cheese and let rise again

Divide dough in half and knead half the cheese into each piece, forming 2 balls. If you wish to bake these free form, place on a lightly greased baking sheet, and press to flatten slightly. (You can also form them into whatever shape you want—oblong, baguette, etc. Just remember the dough is heavy because of the cheese, so it's not as flexible in shaping.) Put in a warm place, cover with a dish towel and let rise until almost doubled, about 45-60 minutes.

To bake in loaf pans, grease two 9 x 5-inch pans and shape each ball into logs long enough so that the dough touches the ends of the pan.

Step 6: Bake

Preheat oven to 375° and bake for 25 minutes. Reverse pans (top to bottom, back to front) and bake for another 5 to 15 minutes. (Loaves in 9 x 5-inch pans will take longer than free form loaves). Check by tapping on bottom. They should sound hollow when done.

Remove loaves from pan and cool on wire racks for at least 1/2 hour before slicing.

Makes 2 loaves.

The Mole Ranch of Elk

Jania Waldman's
Apple Cake Muffins

4 cups apples, chopped
2 cups flour
2 teaspoons baking soda
3/4 teaspoon salt
2 teaspoons cinnamon
2 eggs
2 cups brown sugar
1/4 cup water
1/4 cup white sugar
1 teaspoon vanilla
1/2 cup oil
1/2 cup nuts, chopped

Mix brown sugar and water then add it to all the other ingredients.
Fill a greased muffin pan and bake at 325° for 30 minutes. Test a muffin with a toothpick. If dough sticks to the probe, keep the muffins in the oven until you pull out a clean toothpick.

Elk Cove Inn Bed & Breakfast

Orange Scones

1/2 cup butter, room temperature
1 3/4 cup all-purpose flour
1 1/2 teaspooons baking powder
1/2 teaspoon baking soda
1/3 cup sugar
1 egg, beaten
grated zest of one orange
1/2 cup orange juice
1/2 cup confectioner's sugar

Prepare scones:

In a large bowl, mix butter and flour with a pastry cutter or with your fingers until it resembles coarse meal. Add remaining dry ingredients and orange zest and mix well. Add orange juice and egg and combine until just mixed. Drop 12 equal mounds of dough onto a greased cookie sheet. Bake in a preheated 375° oven for 12 to 15 minutes or until golden brown. Cool.

Prepare glaze:

Combine 1/2 cup confectioner's sugar and 1 tablespoon orange juice and mix until smooth. Spread a small dab of glaze on each and serve.

Makes 1 dozen.

The Old Stewart House Inn of Fort Bragg

Pumpkin Nut Bread

3 1/3 cups flour

3 cups sugar

1 1/2 teaspoons baking soda

1 teaspoon cinnamon

1 teaspoon baking powder

1 teaspoon nutmeg

2 tablespoons maple syrup

1 cup salad oil

14 ounce can pumpkin

4 eggs

1 cup chopped nuts (pecans or walnuts)

3/4 cup dried cranberries

Mix eggs and sugar, blend in oil, maple syrup and pumpkin.
Sift flour, baking soda, baking powder, cinnamon, nutmeg—add to pumpkin mixture.

Blend in nuts and cranberries.

Grease two 9 x 5 bread pans. Pour half of mixture into each pan. Can also make about 4 small loaves.

Bake about 1 hour at 350°, then check with knife in center.

Let cool for ten minutes, then turn onto racks to cool.

Serve with cream cheese.

To freeze, wrap in double foil.

The Lodge at Noyo River of Noyo

Chef Charles Reinhart's
Pain Perdu

2 each eggs
1/2 cup granulated sugar
1 cup milk
1 teaspoon vanilla extract
1 teaspoon grated lemon peel
8 slices day-old croissants, cut in 1/2-inch slices
4 tablespoons butter (1/2 stick), plus butter as needed
confectioners' sugar
grated nutmeg
maple syrup optional

In a small bowl, beat the eggs and granulated sugar until thick.
Stir in the milk, vanilla, and lemon peel.
Arrange the croissant slices in a single layer in a shallow dish; pour the egg mixture over the slices and let stand for 30 minutes.
Heat the butter in a large skillet; sauté the bread until golden brown, about 6 minutes on each side.
Arrange on a warm platter; sprinkle with confectioners' sugar and grated nutmeg.
Nice with syrup.
Serves 4.

"The serendipitous use for yesterday's pastries produces an elegant and innovative French Toast with a touch of lemon."

Heritage House, Little River

Heritage House of Little River

Buckwheat Pancakes

Dry mixture:

> **2 tablespoons sugar**
> **3 cups flour**
> **2 cups Buckwheat flour**
> **3 tablespoons baking powder**
> **4 teaspoons ground coriander**
> **2 teaspoons cinnamon**
> **2 teaspoons nutmeg**
> **1/2 teaspoon salt**

Wet ingredients:

> **6 eggs**
> **1/2 cup honey**
> **1/2 cup corn oil**
> **4 cups milk**

Mix wet ingredients, fold into dry and whisk until smooth.
Butter medium-hot griddle or frying pan.
Ladle approximately 3 ounces of batter, flip, cook to desired doneness.

Whitegate Inn of Mendocino

Caramel Apple French Toast

sliced sweet French bread
1 cup brown sugar
2 tablespoons light corn syrup
1/2 cup butter
1 cup pecans, chopped
8 green apples, thinly sliced
6 eggs
1 & 3/4 cups of milk
1 teaspoon vanilla

Combine brown sugar, corn syrup and butter and cook over a medium heat until thickened, stirring constantly. Pour into a 9 x 13 glass baking dish (spray with Pam first).

Sprinkle with one cup chopped pecans.

Place one layer sliced bread on syrup and pecans: equals six slices.

Top with green apples.

Combine in blender eggs, milk and vanilla, then pour half of mixture over first layer

Place a second layer of sliced bread on top of apples and cover with remaining milk and egg mixture.

Cover with plastic wrap and refrigerate overnight.

Sprinkle with cinnamon and nutmeg and bake uncovered for 60 minutes at 350°.

Each person is served 1 double layer serving.

It can also be served with whipped cream.

The Philo Pottery Inn of Philo

Apricot Strawberry Stuffed French Toast

1 loaf sweet French bread, sliced into sixteen 3/4 inch slices
8 ounces cream cheese, cut into eight cubes
10 eggs
1 1/2 cups half and half
1/4 cup maple syrup
1/2 cup butter

Spread cheese onto 8 slices of the bread and top with the other slice, to make 8 little sandwiches. Cut off any hard crust.

Cut each sandwich into 1 inch squares.

Grease a 9 x 11 glass pan and arrange the cubes in rows.

Mix together eggs, half and half, cup maple syrup and pour over the cubes. Cut up butter into small pieces and evenly scatter over the top.

Bake in a 350° oven for 50 minutes, until browned.

Serve with the following topping:

> **1 12 ounce jar apricot preserves**
> **2 rounded cups fresh strawberries, cut into quarters**

Mix apricot preserves and strawberries together, heat through and spoon over each serving.

This serves 6 to 8 people and is very filling!

North Coast Country Inn of Gualala

Maureen Topping's
Overnight Praline French Toast

1 cup firmly packed brown sugar
1/2 cup butter
2 tablespoons light corn syrup
1 cup pecans, coarsely chopped
12 slices sandwich bread
6 eggs, beaten
1 1/2 cups milk
1 teaspoon rum extract
1/4 teaspoon salt
cinnamon

Combine sugar, butter, and corn syrup in a small sauce pan; cook over medium heat until thickened, stirring constantly. Pour syrup mixture into a 13 x 9 x 2 inch, ungreased, baking dish. Sprinkle pecans evenly over syrup mixture. Place 6 slices of bread on top of syrup mixture. Top with remaining 6 slices of bread.

Combine eggs, milk, rum extract and salt, stirring until blended. Pour egg mixture evenly over bread slices. Sprinkle with cinnamon. Cover and chill 8 hours.

Bake, uncovered, at 350° for 40 to 45 minutes or until lightly browned. Serve immediately, yet holds well on warming tray for 1 to 2 hours.

Serves 6.

The Weller House of Fort Bragg

Swedish Crepes with Blueberry Sauce

Crepes:

One egg plus 75 ml flour plus 150 ml milk equal five crepes. Two crepes per person. Do the math! Pour the mixture VERY thin into a Swedish crepe pan.

Filling:

One cube cream cheese plus 2 cups cottage cheese plus 2 tablespoons powder sugar plus 1 orange, grated, makes enough filling for at least 12 people. Mix thoroughly.

Blueberry Sauce:

Mix 1/2 cup cold water with two tablespoons cornstarch. Heat on stove, stirring sugar occasionally. When it is thick, pour in half a bag of frozen blueberries. (Keep on mid-high until the berries are unfrozen, then on low until everything is used up. Enough for 10 people. Just double the recipe if more is needed.

Roll the crepes:

One generous tablespoon of filling in each crepe. Serve in a V shape with a single broad stripe of blueberry sauce over the top. Insert a small edible and colorful flower such as a mallow in the middle.

Whale Watch Inn By The Sea Bed & Breakfast of Gualala

Breakfast Custard

1 loaf cinnamon/raisin bread (crusts removed)
3/4 cup sugar
1 cup heavy cream
7 eggs + 3 egg yolks
1 cube melted butter
1 tablespoon vanilla
3 cups milk

Heat oven to 350°. Layer bread & melted butter in a 9 x13 casserole pan. Combine rest of ingredients and pour evenly over bread.
Bake 1 hour in a pan of hot water.
Let sit for 20 mlnutes before serving.
Dust with powdered sugar
May be assembled the night before.
Serves 12.

Fensalden Inn of Albion

Lyn Hamby's
Vegetarian Eggs Benedict

toasted English muffin
sliced tomato
sautéed mushrooms
chopped spinach
poached eggs
Bernaise Sauce

Warm tomato slices, mushrooms & chopped spinach.
Toast English muffins.
Layer English muffins with each of the above.
Top with poached egg
Pour Bernaise over egg/vegetable combination.
Stand back, and wait for applause!

Soups
&
Salads

Husch Vineyards, Philo

Husch Vineyards of Philo

Anastasia Logan's
Harvest Squash Soup

1 winter squash*, about four pounds,
    peeled and cut into chunks
1 medium onion, sliced
1 clove of garlic, peeled
1 bay leaf
1 cup Husch Sauvignon Blanc
2 1/2 cups chicken or vegetable stock
salt and pepper to taste
1 dried ancho chili, stemmed and seeded
1/2 cup heavy cream

In a medium saucepan, combine first six ingredients. Simmer covered until the vegetables are soft, about 20 minutes. Meanwhile, combine the chili and cream in a small saucepan. Cover and bring to a boil. Remove from heat and allow to sit covered while the vegetables are cooking.

When the vegetables are soft, remove bay leaf and puree the mixture with a hand blender or in a food processor or blender. Season to taste with salt and pepper. Puree the chili and cream separately.

To serve, ladle the soup into bowls and top with a dollop of the chili cream. Serves four.

*Any type of hard winter squash may be used, for example Hubbard, pumpkin, sweet mama, or butternut.

Complements our Husch Sauvignon Blanc or Chardonnay La Ribera Vineyards.

Bonterra Vineyards of Hopland

John Ash's
Tomatillo, Poblano and Heirloom Bean Chowder

This is a hearty (and healthy) soup with a rich Mexican flavor. Tomatillos add a tart, lemon-lime flavor. The poblanos add a smokey deep flavor and aroma which is even better if you char-roast and peel it before adding it in. Like all chiles, poblanos "heat" will vary so take a little taste before adding in the full amount and adjust accordingly. You can use whatever heirloom beans you want but my favorites are Tocamares Chocolate, Yellow Flageolet or Christmas Lima.*

    1 pound yellow onions, halved and sliced lengthwise
    3 medium stemmed and seeded fresh poblano chiles,
        sliced into thin strips
    1 tablespoon finely slivered garlic
    2 tablespoons olive oil
    2 cups husked and halved fresh tomatillos
    1/2 teaspoon each whole fennel, cumin and coriander seeds
    2 teaspoons dried oregano (Mexican preferably)
    1/4 teaspoon ground cinnamon
    1 1/2 cups diced canned tomatoes with their juice
        (Muir Glen brand preferred)
    7 cups rich clear chicken or vegetable stock
    2 cups cooked favorite heirloom bean
    Salt and freshly ground black pepper to taste

In a saucepan, heat the olive oil. Add the onions, poblanos, and garlic. Sauté until soft but not brown, about 5 minutes. Add the tomatillos, fennel, cumin, oregano, cinnamon, tomatoes and stock. Simmer gently for 10-15 minutes. Add the beans. Simmer to heat through. Correct seasoning with salt and pepper.

To serve, ladle into warm soup bowls. Garnish with chopped cilantro, avocado and lime juice just before serving.

Serves 6 to 8.

Garnish:

**3 tablespoons roughly chopped cilantro leaves,
fanned avocado slices
drops of fresh lime juice.**

Wine Recommendation: The chile heat and tartness of the tomatillos plays wonderfully off of fruity, lower alcohol wines with good acidity and a bit of residual sugar like a California Riesling, Gewurtztraminer or Chenin Blanc. The "new" viogniers from California —particularly Bonterra Viognier—which are typically made in a very ripe style also work here.

*Good mail order sources for heirloom beans are Phipps Ranch (800) 279-0889; Vann's Spices (800) 583-1693 and Indian Harvest (800) 346-7032.

Zack's Catering of Ukiah

Minestrone Soup

This is our family minestrone soup recipe for you to enjoy with family and friends on a cold day.

2 ounces small red beans
2 ounces blackeyed beans
2 ounces chick peas (or you can use 6 ounces /15 bean soup mix)
8 ounces oil
4 ounces onions, finely chopped
4 ounces celery, finely chopped
4 ounces carrots, finely chopped
3 ounces Napa cabbage, finely chopped
1 teaspoon cilantro
3 ounces Bok Choy
1 bunch fresh spinach, chopped
2 cloves garlic, minced
32 ounces tomatoes, canned, crushed
1 gallon soup stock
1 teaspoon salt
pepper to taste
2 ounces Ditalini (or other macaroni)
1 bay leaf
2 ounces sherry wine

Soak beans and chick peas overnight in water. Wash and drain.
Place oil, onions and garlic in soup pot and saute.
Add crushed tomatoes, stock (beef, chicken or vegetable), beans and bay leaf.
Bring to rapid boil. Reduce to simmer and cook for 1 hour.
Add carrots and celery cook for 5 more minutes. Then add the rest of the vegetables, stir, and bring back to a rapid boil.
Add Ditalini and stir.
Add sherry and cook until done. Approximately 12 to 15 minutes.
Remove from heat. Stir well before serving.
Grated parmesan cheese may be served with soup.

Lipinski's Mendo Juice Joint of Mendocino

Spanish Tomato Garlic Soup

For the broth:

1 1/2 heads garlic, peeled

1/2 cup miso (red miso is best for this recipe)

3 cups water

4 cups canned or homemade vegetable stock

Pre-heat toaster oven to 375°.

Bake garlic cloves on un-oiled oven pan until golden, skaking pan half way through, about 20 minutes.

Puree garlic, miso and water, on high speed. Combine with vegetable stock in soup pot. Reheat at low temperature.

For soup:

1 large onion, thinly sliced (I prefer white onions)

1 large potato, thinly sliced

1 1/2 teaspoons paprika

3 teaspoons olive oil

2 cups fresh ripe tomatoes, chopped

1 1/2 teaspoons dried thyme

1 tablespoon lemon juice (fresh is preferable)

7 cups garlic broth

In a soup pot, sauté onions, potato and garlic until onions are limp. Add tomatoes and thyme and continue to simmer for 5 minutes more.

Add garlic broth and gently simmer until potatoes are tender.

The MacCallum House Inn, Mendocino

The MacCallum House Restaurant and Inn of Mendocino

Chef Alan Kantor's
Cremini Mushroom Salad
with Henwood Estate-Bottled
Extra Virgin Olive Oil

1 quart cremini mushrooms, thinly sliced
Juice and chopped zest of one Meyer lemon
1/4 teaspoon salt
1/4 teaspoon freshly ground black pepper
1 cup radicchio, sliced in a chiffonade,
    reserve large leaves for serving
1 teaspoon chopped garlic
3 tablespoons Henwood Estate Private Reserve olive oil*
1 tablespoon pecorino Romano or Sonoma dry jack cheese
1/2 cup red onion, thinly sliced (optional)
Italian parsley, freshly chopped, for garnish

Toss together gently. Place a large radicchio leaf cup on each plate and fill with mushroom mixture. Sprinkle with freshly chopped Italian flat-leaf parsley, confetti-style. Drizzle additional olive oil around plate.

*Henwood's Private Reserve is a blend pressed from Mission, Frantoia and French Picholine olives. Henwood's premium cold pressed olive oils made from hand-picked olives are available at The MacCallum House Restaurant.

Fetzer Vineyards of Hopland and Mendocino

John Ash's
Wild Mushroom Salad
With A Corn Mustard Dressing

This is a pretty straight-forward salad that is dependent on a few special ingredients to make it great. First is to use good mushrooms. Wild and cultivated exotic mushrooms have become much more readily available in recent years. Use the best selection that you can find.*

Serves 6

> **3 tablespoons clarified butter or olive oil**
> **1 1/2 pounds wild mushrooms such as oyster, chantrelle, alba**
>   **or best available**
> **sea salt and freshly ground pepper**
> **8 cups loosely packed mixed young savory greens,**
>   **such as arugula, cress, mizuna, tat soi**
> **Honey Lemon Vinaigrette (recipe follows)**
> **Corn Mustard Dressing (recipe follows)**

Garnish:
    Fresh dill sprigs, fried capers, shaved Parmesan or dry jack cheese

Heat the clarified butter in a large sauté pan and sauté the mushrooms until barely tender and still holding their shape. Season with salt and freshly ground pepper, set aside and keep warm.

Lightly toss the greens with some of the honey lemon vinaigrette and arrange attractively on plates with the mushrooms. Spoon the corn mustard dressing around and garnish with the dill sprigs, fried capers and cheese. Serve immediately.

Honey Lemon Vinaigrette

Makes 1+ cups

> 2 tablespoons finely chopped shallot
> 6 tablespoons seasoned rice vinegar
> 2 tablespoons fragrant honey
> 4 tablespoons fresh lemon juice
> 4 tablespoons olive oil

Whisk all ingredients together. Store covered and refrigerated, up to 5 days.

Corn Mustard Dressing

Makes about 1 cup

> 2 tablespoons finely chopped shallots
> 2 teaspoons poached or roasted garlic
> 1/4 cup double strength, unsalted chicken or vegetable broth
> 1 tablespoon Dijon mustard (or to taste)
> 1/2 cup Spectrum Naturals unrefined corn oil
> 1 teaspoon fresh lemon juice
> sea salt and freshly ground pepper to taste

Add shallots, garlic and stock to a blender and blend until smooth. Add mustard and slowly pour oil in with motor running until dressing is smooth and thickened. Stir in lemon juice and season with salt and pepper. Store covered in refrigerator, up to 3 days.

Wine Recommendation: The creamy, citrusy dressings and the mushrooms are a mirror of the flavors in a rich, barrel fermented and aged chardonnay.

*A supplier that I have worked with for many years in Northern California is Gourmet Mushroom (707) 823-1743 who will ship a beautiful basket of exotics anywhere in the U.S. The second essential in this recipe is the corn oil. It's not the usual oil found in supermarkets but a very special one made by Spectrum Naturals in Petaluma, CA. (707) 778-8900, spectrumnaturals@netdex.com. It's a very pure expeller extracted oil from corn that uses no solvent or preservatives and is absolutely delicious because it tastes and smells like corn (what a concept!). You can find it at health and natural food stores.

Fetzer Vineyards, Hopland

Fish
&
Seafood

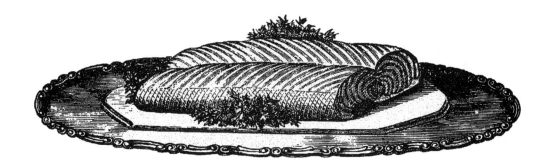

Stevenswood Lodge of Little River

Marc Dym's
Local Pacific Salmon
Prepared Pesto Style On A Bed
Of Wilted Escarole

Salmon ingredients and preparation:

      6 salmon filets, boneless and skinless (7 ounces each)

      1/2 cup pine nuts (chopped fine)

      1 bunch basil (washed leaves only)

      2 cloves garlic (chopped)

      1 cup canola oil

      1/4 teaspoon white pepper

      1 teaspoon salt

Escarole ingredients:

      2 tablespoons extra virgin olive oil

      2 heads escarole (washed and rough chopped)

      3 cloves garlic (chopped)

      2 tablespoons Parmesan cheese

      Salt and pepper to taste

Salmon preparation: Chop pine nuts in food processor, until fine. Season with salt and pepper. Spread a thin layer of chopped nuts over one side of boneless, skinless salmon fillets. Refrigerate until needed.

Basil oil preparation: Puree basil (leaves only) in food processor, adding canola oil in slowly. Puree until smooth. Season basil oil with salt and pepper to taste and reserve.

Cooking the salmon: Preheat oven to 400 degrees. Heat cast iron pan over medium heat. Add small amount of canola oil. Cook salmon (nut crusted side down) over medium high heat 2-3 minutes until nuts are light brown. Turn over and place on a sheet pan nut side up. Finish cooking salmon 3-5 minutes (medium rare) in preheated oven.

Escarole: Heat saute pan with olive oil. Saute garlic until light brown, adding chopped escarole and cook two minutes until wilted. Season escarole with salt, pepper and Parmesan cheese.

For service: Place a bed of wilted escarole in middle of the plate. Place cooked salmon over escarole. Drizzle salmon and plate with basil oil. Dust with Parmesan cheese. Serve with grilled Parmesan polenta.

The Phantom Cafe of Caspar
"If you can find it, you can eat there."

Chef Oscar's
Honey Orange & Sesame Glaze for Grilled Salmon

1 whole orange, cut in wedges

1 1/2 cups orange juice

1/2 cup honey

1/3 cup sesame oil

2 tablespoons cornstarch

3 tablespoons water

2 tablespoons soy sauce (or more to taste)

Combine orange juice, honey and sesame oil in small sauce pan. Heat to gentle boil.

Combine cornstarch and water until smooth. Add to pan, stir until thickened. Add soy sauce. If too thick, thin with water.

Brush on salmon often while grilling.

Right before serving, squeeze fresh orange on fish.

Also good on chicken.

Brutocao Cellars, Hopland

Brutocao Cellars of Hopland and Philo

BBQ Teriaki Salmon

1 1/2 lbs. salmon fillet (preferably King salmon)
   —do not remove skin
2 bell peppers—1 red & 1 green
1 onion
1 lemon
teriaki sauce
1 orange
garlic powder
pinch of herbs
pepper
season salt

Squeeze lemon over the fillet. Baste with teriaki sauce. Lightly season the fillet.

Thinly slice the onion, orange and peppers and arrange on top of the fillet. Allow to sit at room temperature for 30 to 45 minutes while you ready the BBQ.

Place the fillet on the grill, skin side down over the coals. Baste With teriaki frequently. Remove when opaque (it will continue to cook.) Remove from the grill by taking a spatula and going between the skin and the meat. The skin remains on the BBQ.

Serve with a crisp, cool Semillon or Sauvignon Blanc. Complement with field greens salad and fresh vegetables

Serves 4.

Duncan Peak Vineyards of Hopland

Resa & Hubert Lenczowski's
Seafood Okra Gumbo

2 pounds fresh or frozen uncooked, head on, shrimp (40 or 50 per pound)
2 quarts water
2 fresh or frozen crabs
1 quart water
2 tablespoons vegetable oil
1 quart fresh or frozen okra, cut into 2 inch slices
2/3 cup vegetable oil
1/2 cup flour
2 cups chopped onions
1 cup chopped green bell pepper
1/2 cup chopped celery
1 teaspoon minced garlic
1 16 ounce can chopped tomatoes
2 bay leaves
2 teaspoons salt or to taste
1/2 teaspoon black pepper
1/2 teaspoon white pepper
l/4 teaspoon cayenne pepper or to taste

Peel, de-vein and remove heads from the shrimp, reserving shells and heads. Cover and chill the shrimp. Rinse the shells and heads and place in a large nonreactive saucepan with 2 quarts water. Bring to a boil, reduce the heat and simmer for 30 to 45 minutes. Strain the stock and reserve. Discard the shells and heads.

Rinse the crabs well and place in a nonreactive saucepan with 1 quart water. Bring to a boil, reduce the heat and simmer for 20 to 30 minutes. Strain and reserve stock and crabs. When the crabs are cool enough to handle, snap off both claws and break the body in half. Set aside.

Put 2 tablespoons oil and the okra in a microwavable container and heat on high until all the stringiness is gone.

Heat 2/3 cup oil in an 8 quart heavy saucepan over medium high heat.

Add flour and stir until the roux is a dark brown color. Don't let it burn! Add the onions, bell pepper, celery and garlic and sauté until the vegetables are tender. Allow the vegetables to stick to the bottom of the pan occasionally so that they caramelize. Add the tomatoes, bay leaves, black pepper, white pepper, and cayenne pepper. Add the cooked okra, stirring constantly. Add the crab stock and half the shrimp stock. Bring the mixture to a boil, stirring constantly. Reduce the heat, cover partially and simmer for 30 minutes, stirring constantly. Add additional shrimp stock if the gumbo is too thick. Season with salt and pepper. Add the broken crabs and simmer 5 minutes or until the shrimp are firm and pink. Discard the bay leaves.

Serve over rice in large bowls. Flavor improves with time so make it in the morning to allow the flavors to blend. Invite your friends over and serve with your favorite Ducan Peak Vineyards Cabernet Sauvignon and enjoy this old family recipe from Resa's aunt in Louisiana.

Six entree servings.

Pepperwood Springs Vineyards of Philo

Crab in Garlic & Olive Oil

Clean crab. Remove legs from the body and crack ready for eating. Quarter the body. Put the crab sections in a glass or metal pan, or even better an oven-proof serving casserole (I have a lovely oven proof casserole dish made by the potter, Jan Wax, of Philo).

Chop up one half to one full head of garlic. Sprinkle the garlic over the crab.

Pour over the crab about 1/2 cup of olive oil. Toss the olive oil and garlic around the crab.

Bake in hot (400°) oven for 15 to 20 minutes.

Serve with a salad and good sour dough French bread. The bread is dipped in the garlic olive oil which becomes infused with the crab juices. Messy to eat but worth the taste treat.

Ledford House of Albion

Pacific Fish Stew

This stew is served with a crostini and aoili.
Yield: 8-10 servings

> **About 3 pounds of fish (Pacific Snapper, Salmon, Halibut, etc.)**
> **10 cups water (8 cups water, 2 cups white wine)**
> **1 cup diced onion**
> **1 cup diced leek**
> **1 cup diced carrot**
> **1 cup diced fennel bulb**
> **8 cloves garlic, chopped fine**
> **3 tomatoes, chopped**
> **4 tablespoons olive oil**
> **1 teaspoon orange zest**
> **1 teaspoon saffron crushed gently with your fingers**
> **1/2 teaspoon red pepper flakes**
> **1/2 teaspoon anise seed**
> **salt to taste**

Heat the olive oil in a large stock pot, sauté the vegetables slowly until tender, 2 to 3 minutes. Add the water to the vegetables and bring to a boil and cook 10 minutes. Mix the orange zest, anise seed and the saffron with 1/4 cup of the stock; add with the tomatoes back to the stock and bring to a boil. Add the salt and red pepper flakes. Just before serving, bring to a boil and add the fish.

Basic Aioli Sauce:

> **4 garlic cloves, peeled**
> **3 large egg yolks**
> **1/2 teaspoon salt**
> **4 tablespoons fresh lemon juice**
> **1-1 1/2 cups olive oil**

Place garlic in food processor and mince until fine. Add yolks, salt and juice and process until smooth. With machine running, slowly and in a steady stream pour olive oil into work bowl. *Variations-Rosemary Aioli; add a tablespoon of rosemary to garlic, then proceed with the rest of the recipe.

Domaine Saint Gregory of Hopland and Redwood Valley

Mendocino Seafood Soup

1/4 cup butter

1 large onion, chopped

1 clove garlic, minced

6 mushrooms, sliced

5 cups chicken stock

1 cup Saint Gregory Pinot Blanc

1/2 teaspoon tarragon

1/8 teaspoon dried dillweed

2 medium potatoes, peeled and cut into 1/2 inch cubes

1 pound fish fillets (snapper or cod), cut into 1/2 inch cubes

1 6 1/2 ounce can minced clams (drained)

1/4 pound shrimp

1/2 pound crabmeat

1 lemon, cut into wedges

1 teaspoon minced parsley

fresh ground pepper

In an 8-quart pan, sauté onion, garlic and mushrooms in butter over medium high heat, until tender.

Add stock, wine, tarragon and dill. Bring to a boil.

Add potatoes, cover and simmer until tender, about 20 minutes.

Add cubed fish, cover and simmer until fish is opaque.

Add clams, shrimp and crab. Cover and simmer until hot, another 3 minutes. Squeeze in lemon juice.

Sprinkle with parsley and add pepper to taste.

Hill House of Mendocino

Chef James Weber's
Rock Cod Noyo

1 *fresh* filet of rock cod (red snapper)
1 1/2 tablespoons sweet butter
1 tablespoon minced garlic
Fish stock (substitute clam juice if necessary)
White wine
pinch of cinnamon
3 lemon slices

Sauté cod filet with 1/2 tablespoon of butter and remove to plate.

Working quickly as not to let filet cool, deglaze pan with fish stock. Add the white wine, garlic, lemon slices and the pinch of cinnamon. Reduce and set the sauce with the remaining butter.

Pour over the filet.

Serve with wild rice and a mixed green salad.

Greenwood Pier Cafe of Elk

Kendrick's
Ling Cod with French Sorrel in Parchment

Sauté 4 chopped green onions with one bunch French Sorrel in two tablespoons butter, add juice of 1 lime and 5 leaves finely chopped peppermint.

Wrap in 4 parchment squares, 1/3 to 1/2 pound filet of cod with 1 fresh bay leaf and the Sorrel sauce. Fold or twist ends.

Bake at 350° for about 20 minutes.

Serve with Basmati steamed rice and asparagus with almond slivers.

Serve to guests, cutting ends of parchment and opening up the paper for the aroma.

Serves 4.

Mendocino Hotel & Garden Suites of Mendocino

Chef Colleen Murphy's
Crab Pasta Salad

2 pounds cooked farfalle
2 whole crabs, picked
1 red pepper, diced
1 yellow pepper, diced
1 green pepper, diced
1 cucumber, diced
1/2 cup sundried tomatoes, chopped
1/4 cup calamata olives
1/2 red onion, diced
1 pound feta cheese, crumbled

Toss the above ingredients together and coat with enough vinaigrette to moisten. Add salt and white pepper to taste.

Vinaigrette:

1/3 cup balsamic vinegar
2/3 cup virgin olive oil
1 smoked tomato, minced
1/2 tablespoon. minced garlic
1 shallot, minced
2 pieces bacon, cooked and minced

Combine all ingredients and let sit at least 2 hours.

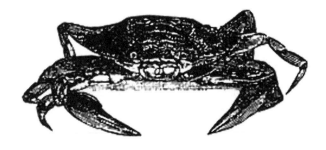

Monte Volpe Vineyards of Redwood Valley

Chef Stephen Smith of Albion River Inn
Steamed Dungeness Crab Dumplings with Lemongrass Dressing and Chili-Garlic Dipping Sauce

Crab Dumplings

8 ounces Dungeness crab meat

4 ounces rock shrimp

1 package wonton wrappers

2 tablespoons fresh minced ginger

1 tablespoon salt

1 ounce heavy cream

2 tablespoons chopped cilantro

1 teaspoon granulated sugar

1 egg, beaten

1 egg white

1/2 tablespoon ground black pepper

1/2 cup Napa cabbage hearts, finely diced

Combine rock shrimp, ginger, egg white, cream, cilantro, sugar, salt and pepper in food processor. Blend until creamy. Place in bowl and fold in Napa cabbage and crab meat. Refrigerate 2 hours before assembling dumplings.

Brush each wrapper lightly with beaten egg and center a tablespoon of crab mixture on the wrapper. Form into "beggar's pouch" by gathering edges together to form a little sack, pressing to seal.

Steam in wok with perforated tray for 8-10 minutes on medium-high heat.

Place on plate with Chili Garlic Dipping Sauce underneath or serve sauce on the side.

Note: Tossed greens or thinly shredded Napa cabbage leaves with thinly sliced cucumbers in Chef Stephen's Lemongrass Dressing are a nice garnish.

Chili-Garlic-Lime Dipping Sauce

2 tablespoons peanut oil
2 tablespoons minced garlic
1 cup chicken broth
2 tablespoons tomato paste
2 limes, juiced
2 tablespoons minced ginger
2 tablespoons minced shallots
2 tablespoons granulated sugar
2 tablespoons chopped cilantro
3 tablespoons cornstarch dissolved in a little warm water
1 tablespoon minced Thai chili or jalapeno
salt and pepper to taste

Heat oil in saucepan. Add ginger, shallots, garlic and chilies and sweat for 5 minutes on medium heat. Add chicken stock, sugar and tomato paste and simmer for 15 minutes. Add lime juice, cilantro and cornstarch and simmer for 5 minutes more.

Remove from heat and serve on the side or under the dumplings.

Lemongrass Dressing for Greens

2 stalks lemongrass
4 ounces chicken stock
1/2 cup peanut or salad oil
1 tablespoon minced garlic
2 ounces soy sauce
1 tablespoon finely chopped cilantro

Combine first four ingredients in saucepan and reduce by half. Pour into bowl and let cool. Slowly whisk in oil and chopped cilantro and refrigerate till needed. Toss with shredded napa cabbage and thinly sliced cucumbers or salad greens, for garnish.

These dumplings pair perfectly with Monte Volpe Tocai Friulano.

Albion River Inn, Albion

Albion River Inn of Albion

Chef Stephen Smith's
Thai Rock Shrimp Cakes

8 ounces rock shrimp
1 ounce cream
1 egg white
1 ounce oyster sauce
2 green onions, sliced
2 ounces water chestnuts, chopped
2 tablespoons cilantro, chopped
2 cups panko (Japanese bread crumbs)
1 tablespoon fresh ginger, chopped
3 ounces peanut oil

Preheat oven to 350°. Combine all ingredients except Panko crumbs in a food processor until smooth. Refrigerate mixture for one hour.

Form into 12 equal size pieces. Roll the pieces in the Panko crumbs, one at a time, until fully coated. Flatten lightly with hands into cakes.

Heat peanut oil in large skillet until almost smoking. Add cakes and cook until golden brown on both sides. Place onto cookie sheet and finish cooking in the oven for 5 minutes.

Serve over tossed greens with Coconut Curry Dipping Sauce (see below) and lime wedges.

Coconut Curry Dipping Sauce

2 ounces sweetened coconut cream
4 ounces mayonnaise
1 ounce lime juice
2 tablespoons cilantro, chopped
1 teaspoon red curry paste
1 teaspoon green curry paste
1 tablespoon curry powder
1 ounce seasoned rice wine vinegar
salt and pepper to taste

Combine all ingredients in food processor and adjust seasoning with salt and pepper.

Greenwood Pier Inn & Cafe, Elk

Greenwood Pier Cafe of Elk

Kendrick's
Meditteranean Pasta with Rock Shrimp, Roasted Garlic, Roasted Red Pepper, Capers, Kalamata Olives, Caramelized Onions, Spinach and Feta Cheese over Penne (or other) Pasta with a zesty Marinara Sauce

Boil pasta until al dente; rinse with cold water.

Roast a whole bulb of garlic in the open; de-skin and mince.

Quarter lengthwise a red bell pepper and skin down; roast over an open burner till skin is blackened. Rub off skin in cold running water. Sliver lengthwise.

Chop a yellow onion and sauté until deep brown.

For the Marinara sauce, sauté 2 minced garlic gloves, 2 minced onions, add 4 cups tomato sauce, 1/2 cup dry red wine, 2 fresh bay leaves, soy sauce to taste, small amounts of crushed oregano, basil, thyme and rosemary, and black pepper and crushed dry semi-hot red peppers. Simmer for two hours.

In olive oil sauté pasta and marinara sauce, add other ingredients, saving the rock shrimp and spinach for last.

Serve and sprinkle with feta cheese and Italian parsley. Decorate with orange and yellow calendula petals around the side.

For 4 to 6.

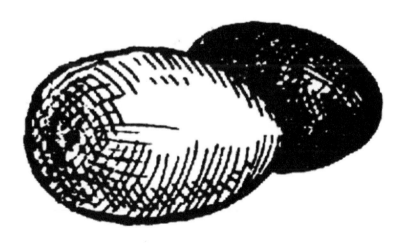

The Restaurant of Fort Bragg

Jim's Pasta

"Have you ever wondered, 'What do restaurant owners/cooks eat?' Well, I would happily eat, every night, a pasta Jim makes for me. I sit eagerly, banging my spoon on my plate 'til the dish arrives. I hope you, having tried it, will feel the same way."—Barbara Larsen

1-2 tablespoons olive oil
I clove garlic, minced
I heaping tablespoon toasted pinenuts
I strip bacon, sliced cross-ways, fried crisp, drained
2 large prawns, peeled, de-veined, each cut cross-ways
    into 4 pieces, dusted with Cajun seasoning to taste
a nice handful Rodiatore pasta, cooked al dente
Parmesan cheese

Heat olive oil in sauté pan. Over moderate high heat, sauté prawns first until pink, 1 to 1 1/2 minutes. Add all other ingredients except pasta; sauté until garlic is softened. Toss with drained pasta.

Top with generous amount grated Parmesan cheese.

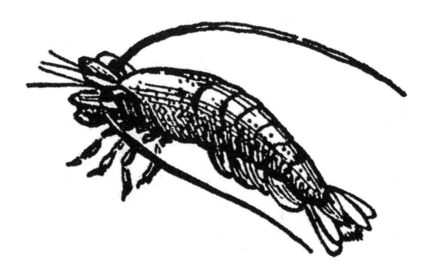

Bluebird Cafe & Catering Company of Hopland

Red Pepper Prawns

5 prawns per person, peeled & de-veined
1 jar red pepper jelly
juice of 1 lemon
generous splash of Jepson Vineyards Chardonnay
4 cloves minced fresh garlic
flour for dredging
olive oil

Dredge prawns in flour until coated. Sauté briefly in olive oil until pink. Add garlic and brown slightly. Add chardonnay, then remaining ingredients when flames abate. Melt jelly while stirring until sauce is smooth.
Serve immediately with a side dish of wild rice pilaf.

Mendo Bistro of Fort Bragg

Chef Nicholas Petti's
Roasted Mussels with Pancetta Shallot Butter

4 pounds mussels, scrubbed and debearded
12 ounces butter, melted
4 shallots, sliced thin
8 slices pancetta, chopped and cooked
1 tablespoon lemon juice
salt & pepper to taste
1 tablespoon Italian parsley, chopped

Preheat oven to 450°.
Roast mussels in pan that will hold them in a single layer until they open. Meanwhile, combine other ingredients over low heat. Pour over mussels and toss to combine.
Serves 4
"Try this with Husch Vineyards' Sauvignon Blanc."

McDowell Valley Vineyards, Hopland

McDowell Valley Vineyards of Hopland

Bill Crawford's
Barbecued Abalone and Bacon Rolls

1 fresh abalone
1 pound, thick sliced smoked bacon
1 cup spicy barbecue sauce
small skewers

Wash, trim and thinly slice the abalone on the bias. Place between layers of a ziplock bag to keep meat from splashing and sticking to the pounder. Pound gently with a meat tenderizer/mallet until tender.

Remove abalone and place a strip of bacon on the top of each piece; roll together and poke skewer through to hold roll in place. Place several abalone/bacon rolls on each skewer.

Brush with a spicy tomato sauce that has an extra dose of fresh-squeezed lemon juice or soy sauce with fresh ginger, garlic and orange juice.

Grill and baste over an open fire until golden brown. Remove from skewer and serve while piping hot.

Serves 4-6 persons.

We dive for abalone on the Mendocino Coast almost year 'round. Of all the ways we cook it, this is everyone's favorite recipe. If you don't have abalone, you can substitute chicken breasts marinated in lemon and clam juice for 4 hours.

Milone Family Winery, Hopland

Milone Familly Winery of Hopland

Jim and Vicki Milone's
Abalone Fettucine

There are two prerequisites for this dish:
1. a good bottle of Chardonnay
(preferably Milone Mendocino Chardonnay)
2. an abalone, fresh from the Mendocino Coast

1 abalone

1 cube butter (1/4 pound)

1 cup Ricotta cheese

1 cup heavy cream

1 cup sour cream

1 head garlic

1 pound Fettucine noodles

1 pound Mozzarella cheese

1/4 pound Parmesan cheese, grated

1/4 pound Romano cheese

Clean, slice and tenderize (pound slightly) one abalone. Pour yourself a glass of Chardonnay after that (you deserve it). Chop abalone into small, aproximately 1/2-inch pieces. In a large saucepan slowly saute´ the abalone in butter and garlic (squeeze through press), being sure to use low heat and not burn the butter. Adding some Chardonnay will help. The abalone will take on a darker color as it begins to cook. Simmer for about 5 minutes.

Add to this the heavy cream, then gradually the sour cream while stirring. Add pepper to taste. Stir in Ricotta cheese. Use more Chardonnay if sauce is too thick. Let simmer while you boil the noodles, for approximately 10 minutes.

Boil noodles until al dente´ and drain. Mix grated Romano and Parmesan cheese with hot noodles in a pot. Then add sauce and mix well. Serve on large platter with parsley garnish.

A glass of Chardonnay, sour French bread and green salad will round out a delicious meal.

Meats
&
Poultry

Lolonis Winery of Redwood Valley

Moussaka

2 1/2 pounds hamburger
3 or 4 medium size potatoes, thinly sliced
1 eggplant, thinly sliced
5 or 6 zucchini, thinly sliced

Sauté in oil:

3 medium onions, chopped
2 or 3 cloves garlic, chopped
2 cans (8 ounce size) tomato sauce
parsley, chopped
a little cinnamon (about 1/2 or 3/4 teaspoon)
salt, pepper and oregano

After sautéd, put in bowl and set aside.

Then cook in frying pan:

Cook and season hamburger, then drain the fat. Put back in frying pan and add the sautéed vegetables and spices that were set aside. Simmer for 20 minutes and turn fire off.

Put in a pan 14 1/2 by 10 1/2, in layers, first hamburger sauce, then eggplant, salt and pepper, potatoes, salt and pepper, and zucchini, salt & pepper. Repeat (makes 2 layers).

Cream Sauce

1 cube butter, cut up and melted. Add flour (about 8 tablespoons) until really thick (use a wire whip). Add milk (about 1 quart). Add slowly still using wire whip and then wooden spoon, until it thickens.

Turn fire off and add 5 or 6 beaten eggs and beat all together with electric beater.

Pour over hamburger and eggplant, potatoes and zucchini—poke holes with fork so cream sauce can run down.

Bake at 350° for 45 to 60 minutes.

Redwood Valley Cellars (Barra of Mendocino & Braren Pauli Winery), Redwood Valley

Braren Pauli Winery of Redwood Valley

Martha Barra's
A Whole Meal

Marinate 6 filet mignon, New York or strip steaks overnight in 4 ounces of Stroh Ranch Marinade. Grill in oven or on barbecue to desired doneness. Serves 6.

Before grilling meat, prepare this scrumptous, nutritious side dish:

Cabbage and Rice Sauté

2 cups rice
1 whole onion, chopped
4 tablespoons butter
3 cups cabbage, finely chopped
3/4 cup Longhorn cheese
1/2 teaspoon salt
pepper to taste

Cook rice according to package directions, with salt added.
Sauté chopped onion in butter until softened. Add sliced cabbage and sauté approximately 8 minutes. Add 6 cups pre-cooked rice. Stir into onion and cabbage. Cover pan and cook over low heat for 10 minutes. Uncover and add cheese and salt and pepper (taste for seasoning, adding more salt or pepper if desired). Continue cooking until cheese is melted.

Serve with Braren Pauli Merlot.

Reed Manor of Mendocino

Barbara Reed's
Beef Tacos

12 corn tortillas
1 1/2 pounds ground beef
1/4 to 1/2 cup oil (as little as needed)
1/2 head Iceburg lettuce, shredded

Taco Sauce:

1 large red onion, minced
2 large tomatoes, chopped
juice from 2 limes
*2 Jalapenos, minced
2 tablespoons cilantro, chopped
salt to taste
   —Mix sauce ingredients together

Spread 1/4 uncooked meat on half of all tortillas. Salt and pepper meat to taste. Warm oil over medium heat. Put flat tortilla in warm oil–when pliable fold in half. Cook both sides until golden brown and meat is cooked. Drain on paper towel (I usually do them all and keep warm). Open taco slightly and add lettuce and taco sauce.

*Optional—If not used, those that want sauce hot can add Tabasco sauce to filled taco.

Martz Vineyards of Yorkville

Grannie's Bean Dish

This is a very low-fat, yet rich and spicy dish that can warm up any winter's day.

1 pound lean ground beef, cooked and drained
2 cans red kidney beans
2 cans tomato soup
1 1/2 cans water
powdered cumin to taste
salt & pepper
garlic powder
minced onions

Mix all ingredients and bring to a simmer, add spices & onions to taste. Serve with hot cornbread.
Fireplace and good book optional.

Zellerbach Winery of Ukiah

Wine Burgers

1 cup soft bread crumbs
3/4 cup red wine
2 pounds ground beef
1 can (4 ounces) mushrooms, drained
2 teaspoons onion salt
1 teaspoon dry mustard
1 teaspoon Worchestershire sauce
1/4 teaspoon pepper
1/4 teaspoon garlic powder

Barbecue or fry as desired.
Makes about 8 to 10 patties.

Parducci Wine Estates, Ukiah

Parducci Wine Cellars of Ukiah

Lasagna

2 pounds hamburger
16 ounces marinara sauce
1 whole medium onion, chopped
4 cloves of garlic, chopped
1 1/2 cups cottage cheese
1/4 cup Parmesan cheese
8 ounces Mozzarella cheese
24 ounces Jack cheese

Preheat oven to 350°.

Brown hamburger and chop onion and garlic, add 16 ounces of marinara sauce and let simmer for 15 minutes.

Mix cottage cheese and Parmesan in small bowl.

Grate Mozzarella and Jack all together in large bowl.

In 11x14 glass Pyrex dish, layer hamburger sauce, grated cheese, uncooked lasagna noodles, then the cottage cheese and Parmesan mix. Layer and end with meat sauce and cheese on top.

Bake in oven for 35 minutes. Cool 20 minutes before serving.

The Apple Farm of Philo

Pork Tenderloin with Peppered Apples

For the pork:

2 pieces of pork tenderloin

olive oil

4 tablespoons Apple Farm Balsamic vinegar

1/2 cup good chicken stock

salt and pepper

Rub the pork well with salt and pepper. Sauté on all sides in the olive oil, until browned.

Place skillet into 350° oven for about 5-10 minutes. The pork will slightly firm up; perfectly cooked means a little pink and still juicy. Remove pork to a platter.

Re-heat the pan, deglaze with balsamic vinegar and stock. Reduce a little until slightly syrupy.

For the apples:

4 Golden Delicious apples

1/4 cup butter

salt

coarsely ground black pepper

Peel and slice apples. Sauté in a large skillet in the butter until slightly browned and tenderish. Salt and generously grind black pepper over them.

Slice pork, cover with sauce, and serve with apples alongside.

Garnish with sprigs of fresh sage.

McDowell Valley Vineyards of Hopland

Pork Tenderloin With Sesame

1 pork loin, trimmed
1/2 cup soy sauce
3 cloves garlic, minced
2 tablespoons pungent mustard
1/2 cup sesame seeds, lightly toasted

In a glass or stainless pan, mix soy sauce, garlic and mustard and pour over tenderloin. Cover and marinate for at least 4-6 hours at room temperature.

Toast sesame seeds on a cookie sheet at 400° for 5-10 minutes or until golden brown. Do not let them burn.

Roast loin in oven (or smoke in Kamato) until internal temperature registers 165-170°. Remove and immediately roll in toasted sesame seeds. Let sit for 10 minutes before slicing into thin slices.

Arrange on a warm platter, garnish and serve with a variety of sauces such as creamed horseradish, mustard, mayonnaise, pesto, or tomato/basil sauce and an assortment of thinly sliced breads or garlic crisps.

Serves 12-20 persons

This recipe is equally good with venison backstrap or lamb loin. Great with the red wines!

North Coast Brewing Company, Fort Bragg

North Coast Brewing Company of Fort Bragg

Mark Ruedrich's
Stout-Marinated Pork Tenderloin with Honey Glaze

2 pork tenderloin—marinated overnight
1 cup organic honey
3/4 cup soy sauce
1 teaspoon ginger or ground ginger, minced
1 tablespoon garlic, minced
2 cups Old No. 38 Stout*
2 tablespoons garlic, chopped
1/2 cup beef stock

For honey glaze:
    Mix well, honey, soy sauce, ginger, minced garlic.

For Marinade: Mix stout, chopped garlic, beef stock. Marinate pork tenderloins overnight.

Grill pork tenderloins over charcoal, basting with the honey glaze. When done, slice pork on the bias and arrange on the plate. Drizzle with warmed glaze.
    Serves 6.
    Serve with Red Seal Ale from North Coast Brewing Company.

*Dark, bitter beers such as stout don't belong in every dish, but used with discretion, can be wonderful as a marinade for rich meat dishes such as this grilled pork tenderloin.

Bay View Cafe of Mendocino

Loretta's Voodoo Greens

1 bunch mustard greens
1 bunch collard greens
1 bunch turnip greens
1 bunch watercress
1 bunch beet tops
1 bunch carrot tops
1 bunch spinach
3 cups onions, diced
1 1/2 cups celery, diced
3/4 cup bell pepper, diced
2 ounces hot sauce
2 ounces red wine vinegar
1/2 cup garlic, chopped
1/2 gallon water
1 pound smoked sausage
1 pound smoked ham
1 pound hot sausage
1/2 pound smoked ham hocks
4 teaspoons thyme
salt & pepper to taste

Clean the greens under cold water, picking out bad leaves and washing away dirt. Rinse them two or three times. Chop coarsely.

Cut the ham and sausage into 1 inch slices. Sauté the sausage and ham hocks with onions, celery, bell pepper and garlic until the onions turn light brown. Add the greens and the water.

Bring to a low boil and simmer for 45 minutes. Add more water if needed. Add the hot sauce, vinegar and fresh thyme.

Season with salt and pepper.

Lolonis Winery of Redwood Valley

Yaya's
Lolonis Stewed Lamb

2 pounds of lean lamb, cut into 1 inch pieces
1 large onion, minced
1 cove of garlic, minced
6 tablespoons butter
2 cups of tomato puree
1/4 cup of Lolonis Zinfandel (or dry Red Wine)
1 whole spice cinnamon stick
salt and lemon pepper to taste

Heat butter in a pot and sauté onion with garlic until golden. Add meat and brown. Add all other ingredients and bring to simmer, covered for 1 1/2 hours until the meat is tender. Remove cinnamon stick and discard.

Serve over Ziti #2 or any pasta of your choice.

Serve with salad: tomatoes, cucumber, scallions, lettuce, olives, feta cheese, olive oil & vinegar.

Serve with sesame bread and Lolonis Red Zinfandel.

"I married into a Greek family whose California history started in 1914. Not only was this family the oldest Greek grape growers in Mendocino County, but my husband had nine brothers and sisters. So in order to fit in as an "Irish outsider" I was smart enough to work closely (without any of them knowing) with my mother in law, Eugenia. She was the best chef I have ever worked with, the fastest, and had the greatest ingredients were hers to use—everything was home grown on the ranch. Her recipes are still my favorite Greek dishes."

"The above recipe, like all the others I have, was hard won. After being married for the first year and hearing my husband Petros say, "It's good, but not like my mother's." Who, by the way, had given me the recipe!! I stayed at the ranch for two weeks and every recipe she made I measured out in measuring cups or spoons. I had figured out that "a teaspoon of this and handful of that" depended on the size of your hand! I serve this dish after Christmas week. It's a big hit with my family."

The Old Milano Hotel & Restaurant of Gualala

Mendocino Rack of Lamb with Rosemary-Mint Infused Lamb Jus

6 four-bone racks of Mendocino lamb
5 pounds lamb bones (or one leg of lamb)
1 gallon water
1 pound onion, medium dice
1/2 pound carrot, medium dice
1/2 pound celery root, medium dice
10 cloves garlic
hefty pinch caraway seed
4 sprigs fresh rosemary
2 sprigs fresh thyme
2 sprigs fresh mint
1 bay leaf
1 clove
1/2 cup tomato paste
2 cups white wine
1 cup merlot or zinfandel
1 tablespoon Dijon
juice of 1/2 lemon (or to taste)
1 tablespoon sweet cream butter
salt and pepper to taste

Buy six four-bone racks from your local butcher and have them Frenched. Season with salt and pepper. Sear. Set aside.

Sauté vegetables until caramelized, then add tomato paste and cook 3-5 minutes on medium heat. Deglaze with white wine and reduce 5 minutes. Add 1 gallon of water and bring to a boil. Skim. Add 2 sprigs of rosemary, thyme, caraway seed, cloves, and bay leaf. Cook for one hour or until flavor develops or vegetables are soft. Strain stock and set aside.

Sear and season lamb bones (or leg) with salt and pepper. Add to stock and roast in oven at 250° for 6-8 hours covered with foil.

Remove shanks and strain stock again. Reduce stock to one and 1/2 to 2 quarts. Adjust seasoning and add Dijon, juice of lemon, and sprigs of rosemary and mint until flavor is infused. Strain again and add sweet cream butter to smooth the stock.

Grill or roast racks and sauce with lamb jus.

Accompaniments may include saffron risotto or saffron mashed potatoes and roasted root vegetables.

Serves six people.

Remaining sauce can be frozen in ice cube trays.

Eagle Rock Gourmet Lamb of Yorkville

Curried Lamb Pie

2 tablespoons olive oil
1 small onion, chopped
1 pound boneless lamb shoulder, cut into 1-inch cubes
2 cups canned beef broth
1 cup dry white wine
1 teaspoon curry powder
Pinch of ground cloves
1 small bay leaf
1 cup peeled and diced potatoes
1/2 cup diced carrots
4 tablespoons cornstarch
1 frozen 9-inch pie shell, thawed

Heat oil in heavy large saucepan over high heat. Add onion and cook until slightly soft, stirring frequently, about 3 minutes. Add lamb and cook until lightly browned, stirring frequently, about 6 minutes. Mix in broth, wine, curry powder, cloves and bay leaf. Simmer 20 minutes. Remove bay leaf.

Add potatoes and carrots. Bring to boil. Reduce heat. Cover and simmer until lamb and vegetables are tender, about 30 minutes. (Can be prepared 1 day ahead. Cool. Cover and refrigerate. Re-warm before continuing.)

Preheat oven to 450°. Pour off 1/2 cup liquid from lamb curry into bowl. Mix cornstarch into liquid. Return to lamb and mix well. Transfer lamb mixture to 9-inch pie pan. Invert crust over lamb; crimp edges. Bake until crust is lightly browned, about 25 minutes.

Serves 4 to 6.

Lonetree Winery of Philo

Casey Hartlip's
Pan-Seared Venison Cutlets

2-3 tablespoons salt
2-3 tablespoons pepper
3-5 tablespoons garlic powder
3 cups flour
2 pounds venison loin, dry aged (deer, elk or pronghorn)
1 cup olive oil

If not already sliced, cut venison into thin (3/4 inch) steaks. Trim any fat or sinew from edges. If meat is not tender to the touch, pound lightly with a mallet.

Season both sides with salt, pepper and garlic powder to taste. Place in a ziplock bag with flour and shake lightly. Place in the refrigerator for about 30 minutes, shaking one or two more times.

Heat olive oil in a skillet on high heat. Don't put cutlets in until oil is very hot! Sear venison quickly (about 1 minute per side) until outside is light brown but center is still light pink.

Serve with potatoes, pasta or risotto.

And don't forget the Lonetree Sangiovese!!

Great Chefs of Mendocino

Kate Ratliffe's
Lapin D'Agenais

Serving Size: 4
Preparation Time: 1:00

1 fresh rabbit, cut in pieces

2 slices lean bacon, chopped

1 bouquet fresh vegetables (carrot, celery, onion, fennel)

1/2 bottle Frey Vineyards Natural Organic red wine

12 prunes

1/2 cup Germaine-Robin brandy

1 dash salt & pepper

2 teaspoons sugar

2 tablespoons red currant jelly

fresh herbs (rosemary, thyme, parsley), chopped

Steep prunes in half of the brandy and 1 cup of boiling water. Let cool. Marinate rabbit pieces in the red wine with the herbs before cooking.

Sauté the bacon pieces until well done, then remove and add pieces of rabbit, browning nicely. You may use olive oil if you prefer. Carefully flame rabbit with remaining brandy, adding vegetable bouquet. Add the marinade wine to cover all the meat, and simmer very slowly for 1 and 1/2 hours, covered. Add prunes, and juice they were steeped in, along with the currant jelly, continuing to cook for 30 minutes more.

If a slightly thicker sauce is desired, remove rabbit and vegetables and reduce marinade until desired consistency is achieved. The rabbit should be very tender and the prunes will have added a sweet richness to the sauce.

Serve with the accompanying vegetables & potato gallette.

"This is a wonderful way to introduce novices to rabbit; cooked slowly with prunes steeped in Mendocino's finest Germaine-Robin brandy! I was taught the recipe by the ladies that sell produce at the Sunday market in Agen, France. It was a regular dish served on our canal barge tour."

Mendocino Hill Winery, Hopland

Mendocino Hill Winery of Hopland

Dorinda Sherwin's
Tuscan Chicken Stew

salt & pepper
2 tablespoon- olive oil
4 bone-in chicken breasts (2 1/2 pounds), skin removed
flour
2 cups chopped onion
1 cup sliced carrots
1 cup chopped celery (optional)
4-6 cloves minced garlic
2 14 1/2 ounce cans stewed tomatoes
1 14 1/2 ounce can low-salt chicken broth
1 cup Mendocino Hill villaMendo Sangiovese
1/2 cup chopped fresh basil
2 tablespoons chopped fresh oregano
2 15 ounce cans cannellini beans

Sprinkle chicken with salt & pepper.

Dredge chicken in flour, shaking all excess.

In a large pot sauté chicken in olive oil until brown, 4-5 minutes per side.

Using slotted spoon, transfer chicken to a larger bowl. Now add onions, garlic, carrots and celery (if using) to pot. Sauté 5-6 minutes. Add tomatoes, broth, wine and herbs; bring to a boil.

Return chicken and any accumulated juices back to pot. Cover and simmer until chicken is cooked through, about 25 minutes.

Add cannellini beans and simmer 8-10 more minutes. If necessary adjust seasonings.

Serve with Mendocino Hill villaMendo "super Tuscan" style Sangiovese.

Mendosa's Market of Mendocino

Robin Goldsmith's
Stuffed French Bread

4 chicken breasts, baked already, chopped up
   (great for leftover chicken or turkey)
1 tablespoon parsley
1/2 pound sliced mushrooms
5 cloves of garlic (or more, your preference)
1/2 yellow onion, diced or chopped
1 can sliced olives
1/4 cup white wine
olive oil or substituting with 4 tablespoons chicken broth
French bread
Mozarella or Jack cheese

Heat olive oil in skillet. Add garlic and onions and sauté until tender, about 2 minutes. Add pre-baked chopped up chicken (or turkey) meat to skillet, stirring mixture. Getting the juices flowing. If it becomes dry, add *a little* chicken broth.

Add mushrooms and olives and the wine. Stir, mixing it all together well—letting the flavors and mixture entwine with each other.

Take French bread and slice in half long ways, scooping out the heart but not tearing a hole in the crust. It's optional, but I love to baste the bread with Italian dressing for more flavors, and so the bread doesn't become too dry.

Place 3 slices of cheese on bottom half of bread, then add chicken mixture on top of cheese. Place 3 more slices of cheese on top of chicken meat mixture, then close the top part of the bread.

Bake for 20 minutes at 375°.

Goes real good with a *light* couscous and fresh melon.

The Grey Whale Inn of Fort Bragg

Colette Bailey's
Chicken With Artichokes & Rice

1 recipe of wild rice mix plus 1 cup plain rice
2 cups of water

Prepare wild rice mix according to package instructions, adding 1 cup of plain rice and 2 cups of water. Cover and cook slowly until most of the water is absorbed. Spoon into 3-quart greased casserole baking dish.

8 boneless, skinless chicken breast halves
Paprika
Salt & pepper
4 tablespoons butter or margarine
2 cans artichoke hearts (13 & 3/4 ounces in water)
1 pound fresh mushrooms, sliced
generous pinch of dried tarragon
3 tablespoons flour
1/3 cup dry sherry
1 1/2 cups chicken broth

Season chicken breasts with paprika, salt & pepper; brown in 1/2 of butter. Put over top of the cooked rice. Add drained artichokes.

In same skillet, brown mushrooms in other 1/2 of butter. Season with tarragon. Add flour to mushrooms, then add sherry and broth. Simmer a few minutes. Pour sauce over chicken and artichokes.

Cover and refrigerate overnight to let the flavors blend.

Bake covered 60 minutes at 350°. Fluff the rice with a fork before serving. Serves 6-8.

Dunnewood Vineyards, Ukiah

Mendocino Brewing Company of Hopland

Circle T Chicken

2 pounds chicken breast, skinless—chopped
1/4 cup butter
1/4 teaspoon cinnamon
1/4 teaspoon cloves
2 teaspoons seasoning salt
6 ounces orange juice—thawed
1/2 cup Red Tail Ale
6 drops Tabasco sauce

Brown the chicken in the butter. Combine the cinnamon, cloves, seasoning salt, orange juice, Red Tail Ale, and Tabasco. Pour the mixture over the chicken in a crock pot and cook 5 hours on low.
Serve over rice.
Serves 6.

Here's your fast & easy dinner to prep in the morning, turn on the crock pot, & done when you return from work. Great one-dish meal.

Dunnewood Vineyards of Ukiah

Janiaks'
Chicken Marinade

1/4 cup oil
1/2 cup soy sauce
1/2 cup lemon juice
1/4 cup white wine
3 large garlic cloves, crushed

Marinate chicken pieces all day or overnight. Spread over chicken and barbeque.

Jepson Vineyards, Winery & Distillery of Ukiah

Marti Williams'
Rosemary Chicken with Caramelized Onions

The flavors of fresh thyme, rosemary and lemon are perfectly echoed in Sauvignon Blanc's slightly herbaceous and citrus character. For this recipe, you will need a large, heavy, ovenproof frying pan with an ovenproof lid (aluminum foil will work if a lid isn't available).

> 3 tablespoons fresh rosemary, chopped finely
> 3 tablespoons lemon zest, chopped finely
> 2 tablespoons (3-5 cloves) garlic, chopped
> 2 tablespoons olive oil
> 4 skinless, boneless chicken breast halves
> 3 medium sweet onions (red, Maui or Vadalia)
> 2 cups chicken broth
> 2 teaspoons dried thyme
> 2 tablespoons olive oil
> 1 cup Jepson Sauvignon Blanc
> 1 cup long grain white rice
> 2 small zucchini, cut into quarters

Preheat oven to 350°.

Combine first four ingredients (rosemary through oil) to make a paste. Spread paste onto chicken breasts, and place into refrigerator.

Thinly slice onions—you should have approximately eight cups.

In frying pan, heat 2 tablespoons olive oil over medium heat. Add onions, cook until caramelized* (about 15-20 min). Remove onions from pan and set aside.

In same pan, brown chicken breasts on each side, remove from pan and set aside (chicken won't be thoroughly cooked at this time). Add Sauvignon Blanc to deglaze pan, and cook down until about 1/4 to 1/2 cup wine remains in pan. Stir in the chicken broth and thyme, heat until boiling, stir in rice and onions, and remove from heat.

Place chicken breasts and zucchini into rice mixture. Put lid on pan and cook in oven for 20 minutes.

Serve with lemon wedges.

Serves four.

*To caramelize onions, cook at medium heat, stirring often. The key is not to brown the onions as if grilling them, but to cook slowly, until soft and golden, caramelizing the natural sugars present.

Munchies—Gourmet To Go—of Hopland

Stephen Yundt's
Chicken Mendocino

4 8 ounce boneless breast of chicken
2 cups flour
1/4 package bread crumbs
3 eggs beaten
2 jars plum preserves
1/2 cup red wine vinegar
2 tablespoons Mendocino Mustard
2 tablespoons Dijon mustard
2 tablespoons olive oil or melted butter

Preheat oven to 350°.

For chicken:
Dredge first with flour, then eggs, then bread crumbs. Transfer to baking sheet, drizzle with butter or oil, and bake till golden brown and done.

For sauce:
In a sauce pan add remaining ingredients, and melt over a low heat, whipping until smooth. When thoroughly heated through, reserve until chicken is done.
Transfer chicken to serving platter and cover with plum sauce.
Serve with wild rice pilaf and a medly of vegetables.
Serves 4

Suggested Wine: Brutocao Cellars Mendocino Chardonnay.

Dedicated to Carolyn Savage.

"A Mendocino regional classic dish served for years at the finest inland restaurants."

Gabrielli Winery of Redwood Valley

Joe Spliethof's
Chicken LaVon

4 boneless, skinless, chicken breasts
3 tablespoons mayonnaise
1/4 teaspoon paprika
2 cloves garlic, minced
1/4 teaspoon ground pepper
1/4 teaspoon salt
4 tablespoons cream cheese
2 mushrooms, sliced
1 green onion, chopped
packaged bread crumbs

Flatten chicken breasts with flat side of meat mallet.

Mix together mayonnaise, paprika, garlic, salt and pepper.

Divide cream cheese, mushrooms and onion into 4 equal parts and place on each chicken breast. Fold over to make a pocket. Secure with wooden picks, roll in mayonnaise mixture, and then roll in bread crumbs.

Place in baking dish sprayed with Pam and bake at 350° for *about* 40 minutes.

Serves 4.

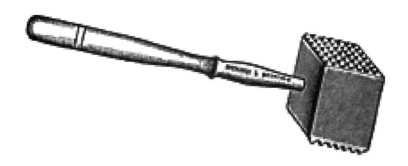

Vegetables,
Grains
&
Pastas

Handley Cellars, Philo

Handley Cellars of Philo

Ellen Springwater's
Braised Swiss Chard With White Beans

1 tablespoon olive oil

2 shallots, minced

3 ounces pancetta or thick-cut bacon

1 bunch chard (half red and half green is nice)

1/2 cup Handley Dry Creek Chardonnay

1 cup cooked white beans

salt and pepper to taste

grated Parmesan

Separate chard leaves from stems. Roughly chop all of the leaves and half of the stems (use the green chard stems if you are using two colors), discarding the rest of the stems.

Heat olive oil in a large skillet. Add shallots, pancetta, and chard stems. Sauté on low heat until shallots have softened and pancetta has released some fat. Add chard leaves; they can be mounded high in the pan, as volume will shrink considerably as they cook. Continue to sauté, moving leaves until all have wilted. Add Chardonnay. Cover pan tightly and cook on low heat for 20 minutes. Check occasionally, adding water if needed.

Add white beans and cook, covered, for 10 more minutes, until beans are heated through. Add salt and pepper if needed, but be sure to taste it first, as some pancetta is highly seasoned.

Serve Braised Swiss Chard by itself or over pasta, topped with grated Parmesan.

Serves 4.

Well House West of Fort Bragg

Jacquie Bainbridge's
Roasted Brussels Sprouts with Garlic and Slivered Almonds

2 1/2 pounds fresh brussels sprouts (about 6 cups)
1/3 cup olive oil
3 tablespoons butter or margarine
1/3 cup slivered almonds
 garlic cloves, minced
1/4 teaspoon salt
1/4 teaspoon pepper

Cut off stem ends of Brussels sprouts and slash bottom of each with a shallow "X." Toss with olive oil in a shallow roasting pan.

Bake Brussels sprouts mixture at 425° for 20-25 minutes. Place in a large bowl and keep warm.

Melt butter in a small skillet over medium-high heat; add several almonds and minced garlic and sauté 5 minutes or until almonds are lightly browned. Stir in salt and pepper.

Toss with Brussels sprouts.

Yield: 8 servings

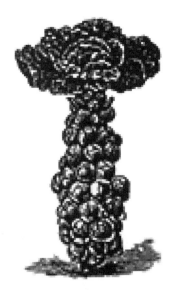

Frey Vineyards of Redwood Valley

Leeks in Frey Zinfandel

6 large leeks (or 12 small leeks)
3 tablespoons extra virgin organic olive oil
2 tablespoons minced fresh herbs
    (tarragon, thyme or basil are great)
2 carrots (cut julienne, thin strips)
3/4 to 1 cup Frey Zinfandel
1/2 teaspoon salt
1/4 teaspoon black pepper

Wash leeks by cutting of the very tops, the old looking green part. Slice through the leek just below where the green tops meet the white base. Open up the leek and hold under cold running water, checking for dirt at the base of the green part, and the top of the white, which is where dirt gathers.

Cut into 4 inch sections, using the younger green part also. Cut the sections in half and lay face down in a glass bake dish. Sprinkle with the juliene carrot and fresh herbs. Pour the wine over the leeks, approximately 1/3 inch deep. Drizzle with olive oil. Sprinkle with salt and pepper. Cover with tin foil and bake until it smells wonderful and leeks are very tender, as there is nothing worse than an al dente leek, or eggplant for that matter!

This dish is superb as a side vegetable to Thanksgiving dinner; and one of my favorites with Pesto pasta and grilled eggplant.

Serves 12.

The Blue Victorian Inn and Antique Shop of Westport

Herbed Green Beans

1/4 cup celery, chopped finely

1 pound green beans

1/4 cup butter or margarine

3/4 cup onion, minced

1 clove garlic, minced

2 tablespoons parsley flakes

1/4 teaspoon dried rosemary

1/4 teaspoon dried basil

3/4 teaspoon salt

Remove ends and string and prepare one of these ways:

    SNAPPED—snap or cut into 1" or 2" pieces

    CROSSCUT—cut crosswise into thin slanted slices

    FRENCH CUT—cut lengthwise into thin strips

Cook green beans until crisp tender. While you are cooking the green beans, melt butter, add onions, garlic and celery and sauté 5 minutes.

Add the rest of the ingredients.

Let simmer covered for 10 minutes. Combine and toss well with the drained beans.

This will serve 4.

Victorian Gardens of Manchester

Artichokes 'Alla Romana'
(Roman Style)

For six:

> 6 medium size artichokes
> 1 large or 2 small garlic cloves, minced as fine as possible
> 1 tablespoon Italian (flat-leafed) parsley, finely minced
> 2 tablespoons wild mint (grows along Highway 1),
>   finely minced
> the juice of 1 lemon
> 1/4 cup of water
> 1/3 cup olive oil
> salt & pepper to taste

Fill a bowl large enough to accomodate the artichokes with cold water and then add the lemon juice. Remove outer, tough leaves from all around artichokes to expose the inner, whitish leaves. With a sharp knife, trim the top of each artichoke and cut off most of the stem at the base. Plunge each artichoke in the acidulate water as you work to prevent discoloration. Trim the artichoke base all around to expose the white, then immerse the artichoke in the acidulated water. Repeat with the other artichokes.

Remove artichokes from water and gently press the leaves from the center towards the periphery to open them up.

Pack the herbs over the dilated artichoke tops and then place the artichokes cut-side down in a pan large enough to accomodate them without crowding. Salt and pepper to taste. Add 1/4 cup of fresh water and the oil.

Cover pan and cook over low flame for 30 minutes. Serve warm or, better, at room temperature.

Herbal Elegance Catering of Comptche

Chef Liz Shafer's
Stuffed Mushrooms

24–2 inch mushroom caps

8 ounces cream cheese, softened to room temperature

3 tablespoons Romano cheese, grated

1/3 cup Gruyere cheese, grated

1/3 cup Italian bread crumbs

1 can artichoke hearts, drained

1 sprig parsley, sage, oregano, and sweet basil, minced

4 cloves of garlic, minced

1/3 cup walnuts

1/2 cup dry white wine—preferably chardonnay

1/2 cup Romano cheese, finely grated, for topping

3 sprigs of fresh chives, finely cut (w/scissors 1/16th inch)
    also for topping

Stem and pre-cook mushroom caps in rapidly boiling water which has been seasoned with salt and pepper with 2 tablespoons olive oil. Heat 6 cups of water seasoned with salt and pepper and 2 tablespoons olive oil. Heat to boiling, then add mushroom caps, reduce heat slightly and cover. Cook approximately 3 minutes. Carefully remove mushroom caps with slotted spoon on to tray lined with paper towels to cool. Place mushroom caps in shallow baking pan stem side up, and set aside for later.

Combine the 3 tablespoons Romano cheese, Gruyere cheese, artichoke hearts and walnuts in Cusinart and chop until artichoke hearts are finely chopped but not pureed. Add softened cream cheese 1 tablespoon at a time until thoroughly blended, then add bread crumbs, minced garlic and minced fresh herbs and cusinart to thoroughly blend. Add salt and pepper to taste.

Using a 16" pastry bag with "rosette" tip, place ingredients (except white wine, cut chives and 1/2 cup Romano) in pastry bag right before piping mixture into caps. Carefully pipe the mixture into the 24 pre-cooked mushroom caps. Add wine to equal at least 1/8th inch depth in your baking pan. Bake at 375° for approximately 10 to 12 minutes. Watch carefully, as oven temperatures vary and the filling is very fragile. It could "collapse" if baked too long or at too high a temperature.

Remove mushrooms from oven and cool slightly. Either serve in pan baked in, or remove and place on platter. Sprinkle with reserved 1/2 cup Romano and sprinkle with cut chives. Garnish with an abundance of fresh parsley, sage, basil, and chive blossoms.

Serves 8–10.

Oven temperature: 375°.

Baking time: 10-12 minutes.

Preparation time: approximately 30 to 40 minutes.

Fuller's Fine Herbs of Mendocino

Arlene Fuller's
Marinated Beets and Green Vegetables

> 1 cup cooked beets, sliced
> 1/2 cup steamed crisp green beans
> 1/2 cup steamed crisp broccoli
> 1/2 cup water
> 1/2 cup Fuller's Winter Thyme or Raspberry Vinegar
> 1 tablespoons sugar
> 1/2 teaspoon salt (optional)

Heat the vinegar and water to boiling in a stainless or glass pan. Add the sugar and salt and stir. Pour the hot mixture over vegetables in a bowl-cover and marinate several hours or over night in the refrigerator.

Husch Vineyards of Philo

Anastasia Logan's
Stuffed Portabello Mushrooms

4 Portabello mushrooms
2 tablespoons butter
2 tablespoons olive oil
1-10 ounce package frozen spinach, thawed and squeezed dry
2 slices bacon, coarsely chopped
1 small onion, finely chopped
1 clove garlic, minced
2 tablespoons chopped fresh parsley
1 egg
1/4 cup bread crumbs

Stuffing:

1/4 cup bread crumbs
2 tablespoons butter, melted
2 tablespoons grated Parmesan cheese

Remove the stems from the mushrooms and coarsely chop. Set aside.

In a large skillet, heat 1 tablespoon each butter and olive oil. Brown two of the mushroom caps, tops and bottoms. Season with salt and pepper. Transfer to a baking sheet and repeat with the other two mushroom caps.

Discard any fat remaining in the skillet. Brown the bacon over medium heat. Once fully cooked, transfer to a bowl with the spinach. Add the onions to the pan and cook until translucent. Add the chopped mushroom stems. Continue cooking until the mushrooms have given off their water and this has evaporated off. Add the chopped garlic and cook 30 seconds longer then transfer to the bowl with the spinach. Allow this mixture to cool thoroughly before continuing. Lastly add the parsley, egg and 1/4 cup breadcrumbs. Season with salt and pepper. Mix well. Mound the filling on the stem side of the mushroom caps.

Mix the 1/4 cup bread crumbs, melted butter and cheese. Sprinkle over the stuffed mushrooms. (The recipe can be prepared up to this point in advance and refrigerated, covered).

Bake the mushrooms in a preheated 350° oven until browned on top, about 40 minutes.

Serve as a side dish alongside grilled or roasted meat or as a light entree. Makes four.

Serve with Husch Pinot Noir Reserve or Chardonnay Special Reserve.

Mendocino Farmers Market

Judy Summers'
Yum Yams

2 medium yams
3 tablespoons butter
1 cup milk or half & half
1/8 teaspoon white pepper
1/2 pound fresh spinach, chopped
2 tablespoons flour
1/2 teaspoon salt
1 pinch nutmeg

Bake yams at 375° for 30 minutes or until done. While they bake, steam the spinach for 2-3 minutes and make the sauce.
Sauce:

Melt butter in saucepan. Add flour, stirring constantly for 2-3 minutes. Add more butter if necessary to make a smooth consistency. Add milk or half & half and stir until mixture is creamy. If desired the cooking water from steaming the spinach can be substituted for the milk.

Season with salt, pepper and nutmeg. Add chopped spinach.

Remove yams from oven, slice open, ladle creamed spinach over the top generously and serve.

Serves two.

Mendocino Sea Vegetable Company of Mendocino

Eleanor Lewallen's
Sautéed Sea Vegetables with Honey, Carrot And Rice

This is a very simple, delicious, and beautiful dish which is complete exactly as is, but can be enhanced to your heart's delight.

> 1/2 cup freshened sea palm fonds
> 1/2 cup freshened wakame
> 1 cup grated raw carrot
> 3 cloves garlic, crushed
> 2 tablespoons butter or margarine*
> 2 cups freshening broth
> 1 to 2 tablespoons soy sauce
> 1 tablespoon honey
> 2 cups cooked rice

To freshen sea palm fronds and wakame, cover with cold water and soak for twenty minutes. Cut the freshened wakame into thin strips. Save the leftover freshening broth as soup stock; it is full of nutritional value.

Melt the butter in a skillet, add crushed garlic, add all ingredients except the rice, and simmer for ten minutes. Add rice, simmer for five more minutes. Serves 4.

Variations:

Use all sea palm fronds or all wakame, one cup of either.

One cup of dried bean threads softened with the freshening sea vegetables may be added during cooking, for a delicious, slithery dish.

Instead of combining rice with this dish, simply serve sea palm and carrots over rice.

Other vegetables may be added to this dish to make a sea palm and vegetables medley. Enjoy

*Olive oil may be used instead of butter with great success.

In A Jam of Potter Valley

Richard Rizzolo's
Dried Greek Olive and Sun-dried Tomato Risotto

5 tablespoons Rizzolo's extra virgin Olive oil

1 cup finely minced red onion

I tablespoon minced garlic

2 cups Arborio rice

1 cup dry red wine

6 cups chicken or vegetable broth

3 /4 cup peeled, diced, plum tomatoes

1/3 cup washed mushrooms

1/3 cup thinly sliced red bell pepper

1/3 cup slivered, drained, Rizzolo's oil packed
   Sun-dried tomatoes

1/4 cup chopped, pitted, Rizzolo's Dried Greek Olives

2 tablespoons chopped Parsley

2 tablespoons fresh Oregano

1 cup freshly grated Parmesan Cheese

Fresh Mint sprigs

In a large saucepan, add olive oil & onions. Sauté over medium heat until soft but not brown. Add the rice and stir, coating the rice grains with oil, for 5-10 minutes. The grains will turn opaque.

Add the wine and stir. Cook until liquid is absorbed. Add the hot stock in 1/2 cup increments, stirring until the liquid is almost all absorbed. Continue until the rice is almost done. Add the plum tomatoes, sun-dried tomatoes, olives, oregano, mint, mushrooms, red bell pepper, garlic, and parsley. Cook until warmed through, just a few minutes. Stir in cheese and serve immediately in warm bowls.

Garnish with fresh sprigs of mint.

Serves 4-6.

Good Thyme Herb Company of Mendocino

Debra Dawson's
Real-Time Risotto with Porcini Mushrooms

Serves four as a side dish, two or three as main course.

> a small handful of dried porcini (Boletus) mushrooms,
>   soaked in 1/4 cup water
> 1 medium red onion, finely-diced
> 1 tablespoon butter
> 1 tablespoon olive oil
> 1 cup Italian Arborio Rice
> 14-ounce can of chicken broth, or 1-3/4 cup homemade stock
> 1/4 cup of dry white wine (total of two cups liquid)
> 1 tablespoon Good Thyme Herb Company
>   Porcini/Italian Herb Blend
> 1 clove garlic, minced
> 1/4 teaspoon salt, or to taste
> 1/4 cup grated Parmesan cheese

Soak dried mushrooms in water and set aside.

In a heavy cast iron or non-stick fry pan which conducts heat well, sauté the onion in the butter and olive oil on medium heat until just golden, 3-4 minutes. Add the rice and sauté together another 3 minutes, stirring to coat rice evenly with oil.

Meanwhile heat the stock and wine in another pan or microwave. Add half the hot stock, Porcini/Italian Herb Blend, garlic and salt, and stir for a few moments to blend. Chop and add the porcini mushrooms, with their soaking liquid. Add the remaining stock, stir well, cover and cook for another 10-12 minutes, stirring once or twice. The rice should be creamy but still firm and chewy.

Stir in half the Parmesan, turn onto warmed serving plate, and garnish with the remaining Parmesan.

To make a nourishing and easy main dish, here are some options you might add to the rice as it cooks:

sauteed domestic mushrooms
shrimp
sausage
diced chicken
tofu

roasted peppers
tomatoes
your favorite vegetables
sliced greens, arugula or chard
pinenuts or walnuts

The Melting Pot of Mendocino

Viva Rellenos Casserole

4-4 ounce cans whole green chilis
2 cups Monterey Jack cheese, grated
2 cups Cheddar cheese, grated
4 eggs
1 cup flour
4 cups evaporated milk
salt and pepper to taste

Butter bottom of a 13 x 13 glass baking dish. Rinse chilis free of seeds and cut into 1 inch pieces or (simply slice chilis in half long-ways). Layer the chilis and cheeses in bottom of dish alternating chilis, cheese, chilis, cheese.

Beat together the eggs, flour, evaporated milk, salt and pepper and pour over cheese and chilis. (should fill dish only about 1/2 full.). Bake in a pre-heated 350° oven for 1 hour.

Serving suggestion: Serve with Guacamole, sour cream and salsa (mild, medium, hot to taste.)

Fetzer Vineyards of Hopland and Mendocino

John Ash's
Cous Cous Risotto with Wild Mushrooms, Pecorino Cheese and Smoked Tomato Jus

Serves 6.

This recipe uses a kind of cous cous known as *moughrabiye* or Israeli cous cous. It is made from the same toasted semolina as regular cous cous but the size is larger and round, about the size of whole peppercorns. There are even larger ones made sometimes known as Lebanese cous cous which can also be used in this dish. They are about the size of petite peas and take a little longer to cook. I love to present this surrounded by a shallow pool of smoked tomato broth or "jus" and have included the recipe for this below.

1/3 cup chopped shallots or green onions
1 tablespoon slivered garlic
2 cups sliced shiitake mushrooms, stems removed
2 tablespoons olive oil
2 cups large Israeli type cous cous
1/2 cup dry white wine
4 cups rich chicken or vegetable stock
1 tablepoon grated lemon zest
1/2 cups seeded diced firm ripe tomato
1/4 cup chopped chives
1/2 cup freshly grated pecorino cheese

Garnish: Grilled or roasted fresh wild mushrooms such as morel or oyster, deep fried basil sprigs and drops of truffle oil, if desired.

Sauté the shallots, garlic and shiitakes in olive oil until lightly colored. Add the cous cous and sauté for a minute or two longer. Add the wine and 1 cup of the stock and stir occasionally until liquid is absorbed. Add remaining stock and continue to cook and stir occasionally until stock is nearly absorbed (about 10 minutes). Stir in lemon zest, tomatoes, chives and cheese and serve immediately in warm bowls topped with grilled mushrooms, basil sprigs and the truffle oil. Surround with smoked tomato jus, if using.

Smoked Tomato Jus

Yield: 2 cups

2 pounds ripe, sweet large ripe tomatoes
4 whole cloves of poached garlic
4 rosemary sprigs
1/4 teaspoon minced chipotle in adobe or a pinch of cayenne (optional)
Rich chicken or vegetable stock
1-2 tablespoons white truffle butter or truffle oil
balsamic vinegar
salt and freshly ground pepper to taste

Core the tomatoes and stuff each tomato with 1 clove of garlic and 1 rosemary sprig. Place the tomatoes in a heat proof pan at least 1 inch deep and smoke them for 15-20 minutes over moderate heat or until they are softened. Discard the rosemary sprigs.

Place the tomatoes with the garlic in a food processor. Add chipotle if using and process until smooth. Strain pressing down on solids. Discard solids and thin to a light sauce or juice consistency with stock. Place the mixture in a small sauce pan and heat to a simmer. Whisk in truffle butter. Season to taste with drops of balsamic vinegar, salt and pepper and keep warm.

Recommended wine: *The earthiness of the mushrooms and the lemon zest would work well with either a rich Chardonnay or one of the Maritage whites. Soft reds such as Pinot Noir, Merlot or Italian Chiantis also pair nicely but I'd cut the amount of lemon zest in half.*

Edmeades Estate of Philo

Tess and Ed Walsh's
Pinot Noir Risotto with Wild Mushrooms and Braising Greens

1/4 cup butter
1/2 onion, chopped
1 cup Arborio rice
1 cup Edmeades Pinot Noir
4 cup veal stock, hot
salt and pepper to taste
1/4 cup olive oil
1 tablespoon garlic, chopped fine
1 cup wild mushrooms, cleaned and sliced
2 cup braising greens, (chicory, endive, escarole)
Asiago cheese for grating

Place a medium sized stock pot on medium heat; add butter, onions and rice. Stir continuously with a wooden spoon until onions are translucent. Add wine and reduce liquid down. Keep adding stock, one ladle at a time, until rice is al dente.

Place 1/2 of the olive oil in a sauté pan on medium high. Add garlic and greens, and sauté until just wilted. Season with salt and pepper and place aside. Place the rest of the olive oil in pan and sauté mushrooms until crispy; place aside.

To serve, divide rice among bowls and top with greens and mushrooms. Top with grated Asiago cheese.

Serves 4-6

Pair with Edmeades Pinot Noir.

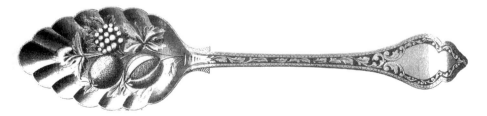

St. Orres of Gualala

Rosemary Campiformio's
Eggplant Terrine with Wild Nettles and Goat Cheese

2 large eggplant
8 fresh organic tomatoes
1 large red onion
1/2 cup fresh basil, chopped
1 cup mozzarella
1 cup goat cheese
I cup wild nettles*, chopped
3 tablespoons sweet butter
salt
pepper
1 8x3x4 Terrine dish with removable bottom

Slice the eggplant into thin slices. Lay them on a sheet pan and sprinkle lightly with salt. Set aside.

In a medium sauté pan melt the butter and sauté the red onion until translucent. Add the tomato and continue cooking for about five minutes. Sprinkle with salt and add 1 tablespoon of the chopped basil. Continue to cook for 5 minutes. Remove from heat and return to the eggplant.

At this point the eggplant can be grilled or baked in a 400° oven until tender but not mushy.

Layer the eggplant on the bottom of the terrine so that it is completely covered. Cover the eggplant with the tomato mixture. Sprinkle with the goat cheese, basil, mozzarella, wild nettles, salt and pepper. Continue this layering process until all the ingredients are used, ending with a layer of cheese on top.

Bake in a 400° oven for approximately 45 minutes. Remove from the heat and allow to cool slightly. Remove from the terrine dish and serve with crusty French bread.

*Nettles are familiar to most people as the source of a painful temporary rash when touched. The new leaves and shoots of young plants under a foot tall are also a vitamin rich, tender vegetable when cooked. If you want to try them, wear gloves to gather them. Fifteen minutes of simmering is more than adequate to destroy their stinging qualities. When you strain the simmered water the result is a wild nettle tea. I gather the nettles at the Gualala River.

Yorkville Vineyards & Cellars, Yorkville

Yorkville Cellars of Yorkville

Penne with Eggplant

2 medium eggplants

olive oil

Italian seasoning herbs

3 cloves garlic, peeled & chopped

5 heaped tablespoons fresh flat leaf parsley, chopped

2 dried hot chili peppers, crumbled

3 pounds fresh tomatoes, skinned, seeded & chopped

9 ounces penne rigate

5 ounces Mozzarella di Bufala, freshly grated

1 heaped cup grated Parmesan

Slice eggplants to 1/4 inch thickness, toss in olive oil to coat lightly, sprinkle with Italian seasoning herbs & grill until golden.

Heat 3 tablespoons olive oil in a heavy serving pan. Sauté garlic, parsley and chilies. When garlic starts to turn golden, add tomatoes and cook about 20 minutes.

Cook the penne in boiling, salted, water, drain and add to tomato mixture. Toss with the eggplant, Mozzarella and grated Parmesan.

Serve immediately with chilled Semillon!

Frey Vineyards of Redwood Valley

Marinated Tofu Steaks With Frey Cabernet Sauvignon, Glazed Onions And Pickled Ginger

For the Marinade and Tofu Steaks:

> 3 pounds firm tofu
>
> 3 tablespoons toasted sesame oil
>
> 3 tablespoons apple juice
>
> 5 tablespoons Dijon mustard
>
> 1 1/2 cups Frey Cabernet Sauvignon
>
> 1 1/4 cup honey
>
> 3 cloves chopped garlic
>
> 6 large white onions
>
> 4 tablespoons soy sauce or Braggs Pickled Ginger
>
> 6 tablespoons toasted sesame seeds (toast in dry sauté pan)
>
> 6 tablespoons thinly sliced chives (or scallion greens)
>
> 12 orange slices (cut halfway through)

Stir together sesame oil, apple juice, mustard, Frey Cabernet Sauvignon, honey, garlic, and Braggs or soy sauce. (For a low fat version, omit oil) Taste for seasoning. Slice tofu approximately 1/3 inch thick, lay flat in bake pan and spread marinade over all. Use your hands, they're your best tools! Spread sliced onions over tofu steaks. Cover with tin foil and marinate a few hours. The longer the better. Bake at 400° for approximately 45 minutes, remove foil and bake another 20 minutes or so, until marinade thickens, and onions are well done.

Arrange tofu on dinner plate, smother with the onions, garnish with pickled ginger, chives, and a sprinkle of toasted sesame seeds. Serve with Spinach Feta Potatoes, Leeks in Frey Zinfandel, and Beets in Sweet Butter with Orange Zest. A simple twist of an orange slice would be a lovely finishing touch to this most satisfying feast!

Serves 12.

For Pickled Ginger:

Peel a fresh ginger root, approximately a 4 inch piece. Slice very, very thin. Cover with a mixture of more or less half rice wine vinegar and half honey (or sugar or sucanat: an organic cane sugar). Boil until liquid is reduced and thickened and ginger is cooked and nicely pickled. Finish off to taste with a squeeze of fresh lime juice. This is excellent with the marinated tofu steaks!

This recipe is very popular with vegetarians and meat eaters alike! It is high flavored and low in fat. Try to get the tofu as firm and fresh as possible.

Another wonderful marinade for tofu is an Orange Ginger Marinade: concentrated orange juice, soy sauce, garlic and fresh ginger are the four basic ingredients. Mix them all together according to taste. Szechuan paste and sherry can also be added to taste. Grill the tofu steaks and boil down the marinade for a sauce. It can be made with chicken also, using same garnish as above.

Tobina's All-Natural Teriyaki of Ukiah

Teriyaki Marinated Tofu Sandwich

4 tofu slices
2 to 3 tablespoons Tobina's Teriyaki Marinate
8 slices of sourdough bread
1 teaspoon butter
avocado
4 tomato slices
4 slices of jack cheese
sprouts

Marinate sliced tofu for 1 hour. Heat in a no-stick frying pan.

Place on 1 slice of bread: a slice of tomato, avocado, jack cheese and marinated tofu and top with a slice of bread.

Melt butter in pan at medium heat. Cook sandwich 2 minutes on each side until browned and cheese melts.

Repeat the procedure with the remaining sandwiches.

Mendo Bistro of Fort Bragg

Chef Nicholas Petti's
Sweet Potato Gnocchi with Gorgonzola Sauce

4 large sweet potatoes
1/2 cup flour (more may be needed)
1/4 teaspoon cinnamon
salt & pepper

Sauce:

1 shallot, thinly sliced
1 teaspoon unsalted butter
1/4 cup white wine
1 cup whipping cream
4 ounces Gorgonzola cheese
pinch of salt
1/8 teaspoon black pepper
2 leaves sage, finely chopped

Roast sweet potatoes in 450° oven until very tender.

Peel, mash and add cinnamon, salt & pepper. Work in flour until dough holds together but is not too stiff. Roll into 1 inch ropes, cut into 1 inch pieces and drop into boiling water. Gnocchi are done when they float to the surface.

For the sauce, heat the shallot in butter until translucent. Add white wine and reduce to 1 tablespoon. Add cream, lower heat and whisk in cheese, pepper, and sage. When cheese is melted, strain through fine strainer.

Heat gnocchi gently in sauce over low heat.

Serves 4.

"We serve these with spiced pecans, a perfect match for a fall meal."

Oz Farm of Point Arena

Oz Farm Scallop Potatoes

Use heavy iron pot with cover.

A mix of Oz potatoes—one pound each of:
> **Red Lasota**
> **All Blue**
> **Yellow Finn**
> **Rose Fir**
> **any other potatoes**
>
> **red onions**
> **garlic**
> **flour**
> **butter**
> **grated Parmesan cheese**
> **1 cup whole milk**

Pre heat oven to 375°.

Slice potatoes, onions and garlic thinly. Place a layer of mixed potatoes, onions and garlic on the bottom of the pan.

Add 6 dollops of butter distributed evenly over layer of potatoes; dust with all purpose flour. Sprinkle lightly with salt and pepper. Repeat until pot is filled.

Add generous sprinkling of cheese to top layer.

Pour milk over top.

Bake covered at 375° for about an hour or until a knife can be inserted through layers. Then uncover and let brown for about 15 minutes.

Remove from oven (careful—very hot!) and let cool for 15 minutes before serving.

The Ravens at The Stanford Inn by the Sea

Ravens Root Vegetable Lasagna

Tender Semolina pasta layered with roasted root vegetables, tofu ricotta with a cashew cream sauce. Vegan and non-vegan.

Noodles:

> **1/2 package cooked semolina lasagna noodles,**
> **cooled and ready to use.**

The Vegetables:

Select from the following root vegetables those you prefer. You will need approximately 2 cups. Peel, slice to approximately 1/4 inch, brush lightly with olive oil, salt and pepper, and roast in 350° oven until tender and slightly caramelized.

> **parsnips**
> **golden beets**
> **onions**
> **carrots**
> **sweet potatoes**
> **turnips**
> **rutabagas**
> **(We avoid lots of potatoes due to the starch in the noodles)**

Combine root vegetables with 1 small roasted red pepper, sliced.

Tofu Ricotta:

> **12 ounces crumbled firm tofu, not silken.**
> **1/8 cup tahini**
> **1/8 cup Umeboshi plum paste***
> **1/8 cup mellow mild miso**
> **1/8 cup chopped fresh parsley**
> **salt and pepper to taste**

Combine in a medium bowl.

Herb Cashew Sauce:

1 cup raw cashew pieces

1 1/2 cups vegetable stock

1/2 cup garden fresh mixed herbs (oregano, basil, parsley, etc.), chopped and mixed. (We vary based on the season and the condition of herbs. For example, we will make a marjoram herb sauce.)

2 tablespoons minced sautéed garlic

2 tablespoons Umeboshi plum paste*

salt and pepper to taste

2 cups fresh arugula leaves

Assemblage:

Layer all ingredients in a 9x13 deep baking dish or individual baking boats starting with sauce, noodles, roasted vegetables, tofu ricotta, arugula, sauce, noodles, etc., ending with sauce for the top. If you wish for the dish to remain vegan, do not finish with a topping of cheese. We offer both versions and are currently topping with Regglano Parmesan.

Bake in a 350° oven until heated through or the cheese begins to brown—30-35 minutes for the 9x13 dish or 10-15 minutes for individual servings.

*Umboshi plum paste can be found in most gourmet grocery stores. A substitute can be made by using a small firm nectarine or firm plum, peeled and seeded, slightly cooked and mashed, mixed with a small amount of vinegar. Umboshi is a salt cured mashed nectarine—giving a taste of a somewhat pickled plum mash. It is expected to be tart.

The Stanford Inn by the Sea, Mendocino

Desserts

Barra Winery of Mendocino of Redwood Valley

Martha Barra's
Warm Orange Macadamia Nut Crepes

Batter for crepes—yields 15

> 3 eggs
> 1 teaspoon salt
> 1 1/2 teaspoon sugar
> 1 scant cup flour
> 2 cups milk
> 4-5 tablespoons butter (divided)
>> —3 tablespoons are used in batter; use rest to oil pan

You may make the crepes a day before serving.

Beat eggs until light. Add salt and sugar and beat until well blended. While blending, add flour, milk and butter alternately.

Melt 1/2 teaspoon butter in a 5 1/2 to 6 inch diameter skillet. Pour just enough batter into pan to cover the bottom thinly when tilted. Cook over medium heat until delicately browned on underside. Turn with spatula and cook until browned on other side. Then transfer to plate covered with waxed paper.

Repeat process until all batter is used, and continute to stack betwen pieces of waxed paper.

Filling for crepes:

> 2 packages cream cheese
> 6 tablespoons sugar
> 1 tablespoon orange zest
> 1/4 cup Grand Marnier, Triple Sec or other orange liqueur
> 1/2 cup macadamia nuts, chopped, divided
>> (use 1/2 cup in filling; use 1/4 cup to sprinkle on top of crepes before warming).
> 8 ounce jar of apricot preserves
> 2 tablespoons butter

With electric mixer, blend cream cheese, sugar, orange zest and liqueur. Fold in 1/4 cup macadamia nuts.

Place heaping tablespoon cream cheese mixture in center of crepe. Fold over edge to make a roll. Place seam side down in buttered baking dish.

Heat preserves with butter over low heat. Spoon over top of filled crepes. Sprinkle remaining 1/4 cup of nuts over top.

Bake in pre-heated oven at 325° for 20 minutes or until barely bubbling.

Delicious served warm with Barra of Mendocino Muscat Canelli (chilled).

Brutocao Cellars of Hopland and Philo

Cabernet Pears

4 1/2 cups Burtacao Cabernet Sauvignon

3/4 cup sugar

1 teaspoon whole black peppercorn

1 bay leaf

1 tablespoon grated orange peel

4 pears, peeled, cored and halved
  (look for firm either Bosc or Bartlett)

2 tablespoons cornstarch

2 tablespoons orange juice

Combine the cabernet, sugar, pepper, orange peel and bay leaf in a saucepan and bring to a boil. Add pears and reduce heat to low. Cover and simmer about 10 minutes. Chill 6 hours or overnight.

Remove the pears and bring the liquid to a boil to reduce by half (10 minutes). Blend the cornstarch and orange juice and stir in to thicken the sauce.

Slice the pears. Fan out onto a plate with a small scoop of vanilla ice cream or a slice of pound cake. Drizzle with the sauce.

Navarro Vineyards, Philo

Navarro Vineyards of Philo

Gene and Anne Duvigneaud's
Navarro Verjus Poached Pears

4 fresh firm Don pears (not too ripe)
2 cups Chardonnay Verjus
1 cup granulated sugar
1 lemon, sliced
1 cinnamon stick
1/2 cup chopped toasted walnuts
1/2 cup whipped cream

Preheat oven to 350°. Skin pears, leaving stem on. Remove the core from bottom without piecing the top. Soak pears for 5 minutes in verjus to prevent discoloration.

Strain Verjus into a heavy pot and add lemon slices, sugar, and cinnamon. Simmer gently until it becomes a light syrup (225°).

Stick a clove into each pear near the stem. Place pears in the syrup, cover and bake until soft (about 45 minutes).

Serve hot or cold with whipped cream and toasted chopped walnuts.
Serves 4.

Greenwood Ridge Vineyards of Philo

Dory Kwan's
A Prelude to Late Harvest Riesling

Ever wish you could have two desserts? You can with a slice of this refreshing pear tart exquisitely followed by a glass of Greenwood Ridge Vineyards Late Harvest Riesling.

1 11" tart pan, lined with a short crust dough (pre-baked)
4-5 unripe pears, peeled (Bosc pears are great)
1 quart water
1 pound & 1/3 cup granulated sugar
1 each lemon and grapefruit (throw in the juice *and* the rind)
2-3 whole cloves
2 tablespoons sesame oil
1 pint milk
2-3 star anise cloves
1/2 teaspoon vanilla extract
4 tablespoons cornstarch
1/8 teaspoon salt
2 eggs
1/2 pint heavy cream (whipped)
black sesame seeds

Equipment: Measuring cups and spoons, blender, 2 stainless steel bowls, whisk, large, heavy-bottomed saucepan, a mixer is optional for whipping cream.

Poach the pears in the water, 1 pound of sugar, lemon and grapefruit, cloves and sesame oil until tender but firm. Cool and refrigerate.

Blend the milk with the star anise, bring to a boil and strain. Combine 1/3 cup of sugar, vanilla, cornstarch, salt and eggs. Slowly add the hot milk to the mixture while whisking. Bring it to a boil on medium heat until the pastry cream begins to thicken. Keep stirring. Cook for 30 seconds longer and then pour it into a bowl. Cover with plastic wrap to cool. Refrigerate until cold, then fold in the whipped cream.

Quarter the pears, core and cut into 1/2 inch slices. Fill the tart shell with the cream mixture and fan out the pear slices on top. Sprinkle with 1 tablespoon of black sesame seeds and refrigerate until the filling is firm.

6 to 8 servings

Claudia Springs Winery of Philo

Fresh Pear Cake

2 cups sugar

3 eggs, well beaten

1 1/2 cups salad oil

3 cups all purpose flour (do not sift)

1 teaspoon baking soda

1 teaspoon salt

1 teaspoon vanilla

2 teaspoons ground cinnamon

3 cups thinly sliced pears

Pre-heat oven to 350°.

Combine sugar, eggs and oil in a large bowl, beat well.

Combine flour, soda and salt in a medium size bowl.

Add flour mixture to sugar mixture one cup at a time, mixing well after each addition. Stir in vanilla, cinnamon and pears.

Spoon batter into a well-greased 10 inch Bundt pan or tube pan. Bake at 350° for 1 hour and 15 minutes. Check with a tooth pick to make sure it is done.

"I make this recipe with Comice pears off the tree in my yard. It is delicious! There are numerous icing alternatives, but we prefer it without icing."

Greenwood Ridge Vineyards, Philo

Gowan's Oak Tree Fruit Stand of Philo

Apple Torte

1 cup sugar

4 tablespoons butter or margarine

1 egg

1 cup flour

1 teaspoon cinnamon

1 teaspoon baking soda

2 cups finely chopped apples

1 cup finely chopped nuts

1 teaspoon vanilla

Pre-heat oven to 350°. Cream sugar and butter or margarine. Add egg. Beat well. Sift dry ingredients, and add to creamed mixture, mixing well. Add apples, nuts and vanilla, mixing until well-coated.

Butter large pie plate or 8x8 glass pan. Add batter, spreading evenly. Bake 35-40 minutes. Serve warm or cold with any kind of topping.

Serves 10.

Apple Crisp

4 cups sliced pared tart apples

2/3 cup brown sugar

1/2 cup flour

1/2 cups oats

3/4 teaspoon cinnamon

3/4 teaspoon nutmeg

1/3 cup butter or margarine, softened

Heat oven to 375°. Grease square pan 8x8x2. Place apple slices in pan. Mix remaining ingredients. Sprinkle over apples.

Bake 30 minutes or until apples are tender and topping is golden brown. Serve warm and if desired with light cream or ice cream.

Oz Farm of Point Arena

Oz Farm Tarte Tatin

This is an adaptation of a traditional French Tarte Tatin. We cut back on the butter (there is still plenty) and heap more apples into the pan than usually called for.

Equipment: heavy iron ovenproof frying pan (9" to 12" diameter), bulb baster, cover for frying pan (a wok cover works well) and a large enough serving plate to turn the tarte onto for serving.

> **12-18 tart (so to speak) apples. We favor Pink Pearl, Jonagold, Ashmead's, Kernel, Spienberg, and Hauer Pippin from our orchards. A mix of varieties works well.**
> **juice and grated rind of one lemon**
> **1 to 1 1/2 cups granulated sugar**
> **1 stick unsalted butter**
> **8 ounces pastry dough**
> **Optional: Serve with whipped cream or ice cream**

Cut apples into quarters. (We do not peel the apples, although a traditional Tarte Tatin calls for peeling). Toss apple sections in a bowl with the lemon juice and 1/4 cup sugar. Let stand for 20 minutes to allow juices to escape, and then drain.

Caramel: Melt butter in frying pan over moderate heat; add remaining sugar and stir until syrup begins to turn bubbly brown. Remove from heat.

Arrange apple sections neatly in a circular pattern in syrup at bottom of pan (remember, this layer will be on top when tipped over for serving). Heap up apples 1-2" above edge of pan. They will shrink during cooking.

Cook tarte on stovetop for 20 minutes or so at moderate heat. After apples start to release juices, baste and keep covered. There may be too much juice released if the apples are very juicy, and you can remove some with the baster.

When apples are all soft, remove from heat, allow to cool somewhat. Then roll out dough and preheat oven to 425°.

Place dough over apples and 'tuck in' to edges of frying pan. Cut several breathing slits in dough with a knife.

Bake in oven for about 20 minutes or until dough is golden. Remember pan handle will be very hot. Place foil or a cookie sheet below pan to catch juices which may spil over.

Remove from oven and let cool approximately 45 minutes. It is easier to reverse tarte neatly onto serving platter if it is cooler.

Reverse onto platter, rearrange apples for neat appearance as necessary and serve.

Etta Place Bed & Breakfast of Willits

Berry Brulee

Heat 2 cups of half and half or heavy cream to nearly a simmer.

Add 8 large egg yolks to 1/2 cup sugar and stir them until just blended using a wooden spoon.

Slowly add in the cream and then strain the mixture through a fine mesh sieve into a bowl.

Cut one vanilla bean in half with a sharp knife and scrape out the seeds and pulp. Add this to the custard mix in the bowl.

Run 3 cups of ripe, cleaned strawberries through a food mill.

Fill 6 four ounce ramekins with a layer of the strawberry sauce and then gently, so as to not mix the sauce and custard any more than absolutely necessary, pour in the custard.

Place the ramekins in a bain marie. Set your oven to 250 degrees and put the bain marie pan into the oven. Bake until the custards are set but still quiver when shaken. This takes about 1 to 1 1/2 hours.

Remove custards from bain marie and cool. Wrap well in plastic wrap and refrigerate for 8 hours or up to 2 days.

Just before serving dust the tops of each ramekin with about 1 teaspoon of sugar. We use a small propane torch to caramelize the sugar, but the broiler also works. When it is a gentle brown, it is perfect.

We serve a little pitcher of the strawberry sauce on the side. It is fun to add the sauce after one has broken into the crunchy brown sugar crust.

Lolonis Winery of Redwood Valley

Thiples

6 eggs
juice of 2 lemons
3 cups of flour sifted with 1 teaspoon baking power
    and 1/2 teaspoon salt
2 tablespoons olive oil
powdered cinnamon

Syrup:

    2 cups of honey
    1 cup of water

Beat eggs into a bowl until fluffy. *Slowly* add lemon juice; while beating slowly add sifted flour, while kneading. Add olive oil and continue to knead until dough becomes stiff; add a little more flour if necessary. Roll dough out on a floured board to the thickness of a pie crust. Cut into strips about 3 inches long & 1 inch wide. Pinch in center of strip to shape like a bow tie.

Deep fry in vegetable oil heated to 375° for about 3 minutes or until golden brown. Remove & set on absorbent paper to drain.

Meanwhile, boil honey and water for about 5 minutes.

Place a layer of Thiples on a platter and pour hot syrup over them & sprinkle with powdered cinnamon. Pyramid succeeding layers until all Thiples are covered with syrup & sprinkled with cinnamon.

Serve cold or hot.

"Serve with a brandy glass of "Eugenia" Late Harvest Sauvigon Blanc, named after my mother-in-law."

Sharon Robinson's
Wedding Cakes & Wonderful Desserts of Mendocino

Mimosa Chiffon Cake

(makes two 8-9" cake layers or one 9" x 13" sheet cake)

4 eggs

2 cups sugar

1 cup canola oil

1/2 cup sparkling white wine or champagne

1/2 cup fresh squeezed orange juice

1 teaspoon orange zest

2 1/2 cups unbleached all-purpose flour

2 1/4 teaspoons baking powder

1/2 teaspoon salt

2 teaspoons orange zest

Preheat oven to 350°.

Prep cake pans or sheet pan by spraying lightly with canola or vegetable oil spray, and lining bottom with baking parchment or waxed paper.

Beat eggs and sugar together with electric mixer (medium speed) until light colored and fluffy. Slowly beat in canola oil, then wine and orange juice.

Sift dry ingredients together, then add a little at a time to batter, beating thoroughly. Stir in orange zest.

Pour batter into pans, tap pans a few times to remove air bubbles, and bake 30-40 minutes, or until cake pulls away from sides of pan and cake tester inserted into center comes out clean.

Cool in pans for approximately 15 minutes, then run a sharp knife around edges and turn out onto rack or clean towel to finish cooling. Once completely cooled, cake may be filled, frosted and served, or wrap with plastic wrap and refrigerate until ready to assemble.

I chill this cake thoroughly, then slice off the "sugar bloom" (rounded top of cake), split the cake layers in half and fill with either raspberry filling, Grand Marnier buttercream, or dark chocolate ganache, then frost with the buttercream and decorate before serving.

This cake was featured in *Martha Stewart's Weddings* magazine.

Anderson Valley Brewing Company of Boonville

Porter Chocolate Cake

1 cup butter/margarine blend

2 cups sugar

4 whole eggs beaten

1 teaspoon vanilla

1 cup AVBC Deepender's Dark Porter Beer

2 cups sifted cake flour

4 1/2 tablespoons unsweetened baking chocolate

1/2 teaspoon cinnamon

1 teaspoon baking soda

1/2 cup buttermilk

Cream butter and sugar, add eggs, beer, and vanilla.
Sift together dry ingredients.
Alternately add dry ingredients and buttermilk and blend well.
Immediately pour into 2-9" wax papered and greased cake pans.
Bake in 350° oven for 35 minutes.

Chocolate Chip Porter Frosting

1 pound semi-sweet chocolate chips

2 tablespoons butter/margarine blend

4 tablespoons AVBC Deepender's Dark Porter Beer

4 tablespoons milk

Soften chocolate chips and butter in a double boiler with only 1 inch of water in bottom. If water is high enough to touch the pan, the chocolate will break.
Combine Porter and milk.
Remove chocolate from heat, leaving broiler together so top stays steaming. Beat and slowly add porter and milk until soft and shiny. Remove top broiler and allow frosting to cool until firm enough to frost a cake.

Scharffen Berger Chocolate Maker

Rich Chocolate Cake

1 cup salted butter

9 ounces Scharffen Berger 62% semisweet chocolate

6 eggs

3/4 cup granulated sugar

3/8 cup brown sugar

3/8 cup cake flour

3 tablespoons finely grated almonds

1/2 teaspoon cream of tartar

Preheat oven to 375°.

Butter the sides and bottom of an 8-inch or 9-inch springform pan. Line the bottom with parchment or waxed paper and flour the pan.

Melt the butter in a double boiler. Chop the chocolate into coarse pieces and add to the butter. It should not get much hotter than 115°. Set aside.

Separate the eggs and beat the sugars into the egg yolks until just mixed. While the chocolate is still warm, whisk the egg mixture into it, then stir in the flour and the almonds. If the combined mixture has cooled, warm it over low heat, stirring constantly, until it is barely warm.

Warm the egg whites slightly by swirling them in a bowl above a gas flame or over hot water (the whites will beat to a greater volume when warmed). Add the cream of tartar to the egg whites and beat until they look creamy and form rounded peaks. Spread the egg whites over the chocolate mixture and fold them together quickly without deflating the whites.

Pour into the prepared pan and bake for 30 to 40 minutes, or until the cake is completely set around the sides, but still has a soft and creamy circle, about 6 inches across, in the center. The cake will rise and crack around the edge and separate from the softer center. The center should wiggle just slightly when you shake the pan gently.

Cool thoroughly in the pan.

To serve the cake, turn it out, peel the paper off the bottom, and drizzle with chocolate glaze or sprinkle lightly with powdered sugar. The cake keeps very well, if not iced, for three or four days. Do not refrigerate or freeze, just cover the pan with foil until ready to use.

The MacCallum House Restaurant
and Grey Whale Bar & Cafe of Mendocino

Chef Alan Kantor's
Raspberry Cheesecake Souffle with Warm Chocolate Fudge Sauce

For Base:

> 1 cup raspberries, fresh or frozen
> 1 tablespoon sweet butter
> 1-1/2 tablespoon all-purpose flour
> 1/2 cup milk
> 2 ounces Gina Marie cream cheese
> 2 tablespoons sour cream
> 4 tablespoons sugar

Mix raspberries with 2 tablespoons sugar and cook over a low flame until it reduces to 1/4 cup. Set aside.

Melt butter in a saucepan; add flour and stir until smooth. Cook over a low flame for 2 minutes, stirring constantly. Add raspberries, milk, 2 tablespoons sugar, sour cream and cream cheese. Whisk over medium heat until smooth and bubbling for approximately two minutes. Set aside and let cool slightly.

> 4 egg whites
> 2 egg yolks
> 1/4 teaspoon cream of tartar
> 2 tablespoons sugar

Separate eggs, placing egg yolks in medium-size bowl. Set aside.

Whip egg whites with cream of tartar until foamy. If using mixer, let run while you prepare the souffle dishes and finish the base.

Liberally butter 6 individual souffle dishes (6 ounce) and coat with sugar. Refrigerate. (Alternately, you can use a 1-quart souffle dish)

Warm base briefly over low heat and mix thoroughly with egg yolks; set aside.

Turn up mixer and continue to whip egg whites to soft peaks and add 2 tablespoons sugar. Whip until soft and shiny and the whites hold their peaks. Fold 1/3 of the egg white mixture into the base and yolk mixture and then put back on top of remaining whites and fold together.

Fill molds flush with top of souffle dish, smoothing with the blade of a knife and running your thumb around edge to make a "hat" or just pile it softly. (Souffles can be made ahead of time and stored in the refrigerator for 4-5 hours.)

Bake at 425° for approximately 14 minutes for individual souffles or at 375° for 30 minutes for the 1 quart souffle. To check for doneness, barely tap the side of the souffle dish; it should wobble only slightly.

Dust tops with sifted powdered sugar and serve immediately with warm fudge sauce. Souffles wait for no one!

Warm Fudge Sauce

1/4 pound semi-sweet chocolate

3 tablespoons sweet butter

1/2 cup sugar

1/2 cup corn syrup

2 tablespoons water

Melt chocolate and butter in a double boiler. Whisk smooth and add rest of ingredients. Continue heating until sugar is dissolved.

Makes 6 individual souffles or 1 quart souffle and 10 ounces fudge sauce

161

Ledford House of Albion

Chocolate Truffle Torte
with Raspberry and Chantilly Cream

16 ounces bittersweet chocolate

1/4 cup dark rum

1 1/2 teaspoons espresso

2/3 cup walnuts

1/4 cup confectioners sugar

1/4 teaspoon salt

14 tablespoons softened butter (1 & 1/3 sticks)

3/4 cup sugar

5 large eggs, separated

2 teaspoons vanilla extract

1 1/4 cups cake flour

Position a rack in the center of oven and pre-heat to 350°. Butter a 10" round cake pan and dust with flour.

In the top of a double boiler, over hot—not boiling—water, melt chocolate with the rum and espresso powder, stirring frequently until smooth. Remove top of double boiler and cool chocolate mixture until tepid.

In a food processor fitted with steel blade combine the walnuts and confectioners sugar and process for 10-20 seconds or until walnuts are coarsley ground. Add the flour and salt and pulse four or five times until blended.

Transfer the nut flour mixture to medium bowl. With an electric mixer beat butter with the granulated sugar for two minutes or until creamy, add the egg yolks and vanilla and beat 50 to 60 seconds longer or until light in color. Blend in melted chocolate.

In another bowl beat egg whites until they begin to form soft peaks. Fold in 1/3 of the egg whites along with 1/3 of the walnut flour mixture into the chocolate mixture continue until the remainder of nut flour mixture is used. Scrape batter evenly into prepared pan and bake for 30 to 35 minutes. Do not overbake.

Raspberry Coulis

2 baskets fresh raspberries
1/4 cup powdered sugar

Pureé raspberries in food processor until smooth; run through fine sieve to remove seeds. Sweeten to taste with powdered sugar.

Chantilly Cream

1 cup whipping cream
1/4 cup powdered sugar
1 teaspoon vanilla

Combine ingredients in mixer and whip until soft peaks form.
To serve, spoon raspberry sauce onto plate, place slice of torte in sauce and top with chantilly cream.

Alegria Inn of Mendocino

Alegria's Most-Favored Cookies

1 cup unsalted butter

3/4 cup sugar

1 cup brown sugar

2 eggs

1 teaspoon vanilla

1 teaspoon baking soda

1 teaspoon cinnamon

1/2 teaspoon salt

1 cup oatmeal

2 cups semi-sweet chocolate chips

1/2 cup dried cranberries

1/2 cup dried apricots, chopped

Pre-heat oven to 375°.

Cream together butter, sugar and brown sugar. Add eggs and vanilla and mix well. Add baking soda, cinnamon and salt and blend thoroughly. Fold in oatmeal, chocolate chips, cranberries and apricots.

Drop dough by teaspoonfuls onto non-stick or greased cookie sheets.

Bake 8-10 minutes. Cool on racks.

Yield: 60 cookies.

Germain-Robin Alambic Brandy of Ukiah

Denise Niderost's
Brandy Snaps

Cookies:

> 1/2 cup packed brown sugar
>
> 1/3 cup melted butter
>
> 1/4 cup dark corn syrup (or light molasses)
>
> 1 tablespoon Germain-Robin Brandy
>
> 3/4 cup flour
>
> 1/2 teaspoon ground ginger
>
> 1/2 teaspoon ground nutmeg

Pre-heat oven to 350°.

Line cookie sheet with heavy foil. Grease the foil.

Stir together brown sugar, butter, corn syrup and brandy.

Stir in flour, ginger & nutmeg.

Drop batter from teaspoon 3 inches apart onto cookie sheet.

Bake only 4 or five cookies at a time. Bake at 350° for 5-6 minutes until bubbly & golden brown.

Cool cookies 2 minutes until set. At this point cookies are still pliable and you can wrap around the greased handle of a wooden spoon (for cornucopia) or shape over bottom of juice glass (for little cup). If cookies harden before shaped re-heat in oven 1 minute. When cookie is firm on mold, take off and allow to cool completely on wire rack.

Just before serving, spoon filling into decorating bag with star tip. Pipe filling into each cookie. If desired tie a thin ribbon (lace is good) around each cookie.

Makes 54 cookies.

Filling:

> 2 cups whipping cream
>
> 1/4 cup sifted powdered sugar
>
> 2 tablespoons Germain-Robin Brandy

In a chilled bowl beat ingredients with chilled beaters at low speed until stiff peaks form.

Makes 4 cups.

Blackberry Inn of Mendocino

Chocolate Date Nut Drop Cookies

Beat well:

> **4 cups of granulated sugar**
> **1/2 pound of butter**

Add & beat well:

> **6 eggs**
> **1 tablespoon vanilla**
> **1 cup + 1 tablespoon cocoa (unsweetened)**
> **1 1/2 cup water**

Sift together & add to butter mixture:

> **5 cups flour**
> **1 1/2 tablespoons baking powder**
> **2 teaspoons salt**

Fold in:

> **2 cups chopped walnuts**
> **2 cups diced dates**

Drop by tablespoons full on lightly greased cookie sheets.
Bake at 375° for about 8 minutes.
Makes about 8 dozen cookies.

Scharffen Berger Chocolate Maker

Double Chocolate Cookies

1/3 cup all-purpose flour
1/4 teaspoon baking powder
1/4 teaspoon salt
9.7 ounces (1 box) Scharffen Berger 99% unsweetened chocolate
  (6 ounces to melt and remainder broken into small chunks)
1/4 cup unsalted butter
2 large eggs, at room temperature
1 1/3 cups sugar
1 1/2 teaspoons finely ground coffee
1 teaspoon pure vanilla extract
1/2 cup walnut pieces (optional)

Preheat the oven to 350°.

Mix the flour, baking powder, and salt together and set aside.

In a double boiler, melt the butter and 6 ounces of the chocolate over simmering water. Stir occasionally until mixture is smooth. Remove from heat.

In the meantime, use an electric mixer on high speed to beat together the eggs, sugar, coffee, and vanilla. Beat for 10 minutes until the mixture is thick.

Turn the mixer down to low speed and slowly add the warm butter and chocolate mixture. Scrape down the bowl and mix until just incorporated.

Add the dry ingredients and the chocolate chunks (and walnuts, if desired) and mix thoroughly by hand.

Line two large baking sheets with parchment paper. Drop the dough, in heaping tablespoons, two inches apart onto the sheets. Bake for 12 minutes total. Rotate the sheets from top to bottom and front to back halfway through baking. Be sure not to overbake. Remove from pan with a metal spatula and cool on racks.

Makes about twenty-four 2 to 3 inch cookies. Cookies keep for two days at room temperature and for a month if frozen.

Mendocino Cookie Company of Mendocino & Fort Bragg

Double Fudge Walnut Brownie Cookies

2 cups all-purpose flour
3/4 cup unsweetened cocoa
1 teaspoon baking soda
1/2 teaspoon salt
1 stick margarine & 1 1/2 sticks butter, softened
1 1/4 cups white sugar & 3/4 cup light brown sugar
   (we use C&H sugar)
2 eggs
2 teaspoons pure vanilla extract
1 10-ounce package chocolate chips
   (we like Guittard chocolate)
1 cup chopped walnuts

Heat oven to 400°.

In a medium size bowl whisk together flour, cocoa, baking soda and salt.

In a large mixer bowl combine the sugar, butter and margarine, beat on high speed until light and fluffy. Add eggs and vanilla, beating again until fluffy. Gradually add the flour mixture, beating well. Mix in the chips and walnuts.

Drop by rounded teaspoons onto an ungreased cookie sheet. Bake 8 to 9 minutes ... careful not to over bake.

Makes about 48 chewy cookies.

Note: We find that cane sugar keeps our cookies thick and chewy, whereas beet sugar makes them flatten out.

By the way, these cookies are great with red wine.

Pacific Star Winery, Fort Bragg

Contributors & Addresses
Wineries

Barra of Mendocino (Redwood Valley Vineyards), 7051 North State Street, Box 196, Redwood Valley, 95470
—485-0322/Fax 485-6784/rvv@pacific.net/www.barraofmendocino.com

Braren Pauli Winery (Redwood Valley Vineyards), 7051 North State Street, Redwood Valley, 95470—485-0322/Fax 485-6784/www.brarenpauli.com

Brutocao Cellars: Hopland Tasting Room, 13500 South Highway 101, Hopland, 95449—(800) 433-3689/744-1664/Fax 744-1046/www.brutocaocellars.com
—Anderson Valley Tasting Room, 7000 Highway 128, Philo, 95466—895-2152

Christine Woods Vineyards, 3155 Highway 128, Box 312, Philo, 95466
—895-2115/Fax 895-2748/sales@christinewoods.com/www.christinewoods.com

Claudia Springs Winery, 2160 Guntly Road, Box 348, Philo 95466—(800) 734-2160/Tel & Fax 895-3926/info@claudiasprings.com/www.claudiasprings.com
—Tasting Room 1810-B Highway 128 at Floodgate—895-3993

Domaine Saint Gregory/Monte Volpe Vineyards/Fattoria Enotria, 1170 Bel Arbres Road, Redwood Valley, 95470—485-9463/Fax 485-9742—Tasting Room 13251 South Highway 101, Suite 3, Hopland, 95449—744-8466/Fax744-8470

Duncan Peak Vineyards, 14500 Mountain House Road, Box 358, Hopland 95449—744-1129/Business Tel & Fax (925) 283-3632/wine@duncanpeak.com/ www.duncanpeak.com

Dunnewood Vineyards, 2399 North State Street, Ukiah 95482
—462-2987/462-2985/Fax 462-0323

Edmeades Estate, 5500 Highway 128, Philo, 95466
—895-3232/Fax 895-3237/kjwines@kj.com/www.kj.com

Elizabeth Vineyards, 8591 Colony Drive, Redwood Valley, 95470
—485-0957/463-2662/Fax 462-4347
—Tasting Room 13420 South Highway 101, Hopland, 95449—744-1302

Fetzer Vineyards/Bonterra Vineyards, 13601 East Side Road, P. O. Box 611, Hopland, 95449—(800) 846-8637/744-1250/Fax 744-1439/fetzer@fetzer.com/ www.fetzer.com/bonterra@bonterra.com/www.bonterra.com
—Mendocino Tasting Room, 45070 Main Street, Box 144, Mendocino 95460
—(800) 860-3347/937-6190/Fax 937-6193

Fife "Redhead" Vineyards/Ca' Vesta, 3620 Road B, Redwood Valley, 95470
—485-0323/Fax 485-0832/info@fifevineyards.com/www.fifevineyards.com

Frey Vineyards, LTD., 14000 Tomki Road, Redwood Valley, 95470
—(800) 760-3739/485-5177/Fax 485-7875/info@freywine.com/www.freywine.com

Gabrielli Winery, 10950 West Road, Redwood Valley 95470—485-1221/ Fax 485-1225/gabrielli_winery@yahoo.com/www.gabrielliwinery.com

Germain-Robin/Alambic, Inc., 3001 South State Street #35, Box 1059, Ukiah, 95482—462-0314/Fax 462-8103

Greenwood Ridge Vineyards, 5501 Highway 128, Philo, 95466—895-2002/ Fax 895-2001/everybody@greenwoodridge.com/www.greenwoodridge.com

Handley Cellars, 3151 Highway 128, Box 66, Philo, 95466—(800) 733-3151/ 895-3876/Fax 895-2603/info@handleycellars.com/www.handleycellars.com

Hidden Cellars/Zingaro/SketchBook, 13251 #2 South Highway 101, Hopland, 95449—(800) 884-9302/744-8590/Fax 744-8592

Husch Vineyards, 4400 Highway 128, Philo, 95466—(800) 55-Husch/895-3216/ Fax 895-2068/tastingroom@huschvineyards.com/www.huschvineyards.com

Jepson Vineyards, 10400 South Highway 101, Ukiah, 95482—(800) 516-7342/ 468-8936/Fax 468-0362/info@jepsonwine.com/www.jepsonwine.com

Lazy Creek Vineyards, 4741 Highway 128, P. O. Box 176, Philo, 95466 —895-3623/Fax 895-9226/lazycreek1@aol.com/www.lazycreekvineyards.com

Lolonis Winery, 1905 Road D, Redwood Valley, 95470—(925) 938-8066/ Fax (925) 938-8069/lolonis@pacbell.net/www.lolonis.com

Lonetree Winery, Box 401, Philo, 95466 —(888) MTN-WINE/895-3228/CHZin@aol.com/www.lonetreewine.com

Martz Vineyards, 20799 Highway 128, Yorkville, 95494 —895-3001/Fax 895-3437/lmartz@pacific.net/www.martzwine.com

McDowell Valley Vineyards, 3811 Highway 175, Box 449, Hopland, 95449— 744-1053/Fax 744-1826/mcdowell@mcdowellsyrah.com/www.mcdowellsyrah.com

Mendocino Hill Winery, 9801 Eastside Rd. Box 749, Hopland, 95449 —468-5570/Fax 468-5562/rsherwin@saber.net/www.mendocinohill.com —Tasting Room 13420 South Highway 101 Hopland, 95449—744-1302

Milone Family Winery, 14594 South Highway 101, Hopland, 95449 —(800) 564-2582/744-1396/Fax 744-1138/milano@pacific.net

Navarro Vineyards, 5601 Highway 128, Box 47, Philo, 95466—(800) 537-9463/ 895-3686/Fax (707)895-3647/sales@navarrowine.com/www.navarrowine.com

Pacific Echo Cellars, 8501 Highway 128, Box 365, Philo, 95466 —(800) 824-7754/895-2957/Fax 895-2758/www.pacific-echo.com

Pacific Star Winery, 33000 North Highway 1, Fort Bragg, 95437 (12 miles north of Ft. Bragg)—964-1155/Fax 964-1105/pacstar@mcn.org

Parducci Wine Estates, 501 Parducci Road, Ukiah, 95482—(888) 362-9463/ 462-9463/Fax 462-7260/tastingroom@parducci.com/www.parducci.com

Pepperwood Springs Vineyards, 1200 Holmes Ranch Road. Box 2, Philo, 95466—Tel & Fax 895-2920/pwspn@pacific.net/www.pepperwoodsprings.com

Roederer Estate, 4501 Highway 128, Philo, 95466 —895-2288/895-2120/info@roederer-estate.com/www.roederer-estate.com

Stimson Lane, Box 443, Hopland, 95449—744-2200

Whaler Vineyards, 6200 Eastside Road, Ukiah, 95482—462-6355

Yorkville Vineyards & Cellars, 25701 Highway 128, Box 3, Yorkville, 95494 —894-9177/Fax 894-2426/yvcellars@pacific.net/www.yorkville-cellars.com

Zellerbach Winery, 2350 McNab Ranch Road, Ukiah, 95482 —462-2423/Fax 707) 462-9263/zinboy@pacific.net

*

Mendocino Winegrowers Alliance, Box 1409, Ukiah, 95482-1409—468-9886/ Fax (707-468-9887/mwa@mendowine com/www.mendowine.com

Breweries

Anderson Valley Brewing Company, Box 505, 17700 Boonville Road, Boonville, 95415—895-2337/Fax 895-2353/www.avbc.com

Mendocino Brewing Company—Box 400, Hopland, 95449
—744-1015/mendobrew@mendobrew.com/www.mendobrew.com
—Tavern: Hopland Brewery, 13352 S. Highway 101, Hopland—744-1361

North Coast Brewing Company, 455 North Main, Fort Bragg, 95437
—964-2739/Fax 964-8768/redseal@mcn.org/www.ncoast-brewing.com
—Tap Room & Grill: 444 North Main, Fort Bragg, 95437—964-3400

Ukiah Brewing Company & Restaurant—102 South State Street, Ukiah, 95482
—Tel & Fax 468-5898/els@ukiahbrewingco.com/www.ukiahbrewingco.com

Restaurants, Inns and Culinary Resources

Albion River Inn, 3790 North Highway 1, Box 100, Albion, 95410
—(800) 479-7944/937-1919/ari@mcn.org/www.albionriverinn.com

Alegria Inn, 44781 Main Street, Box 803, Mendocino, 95460—(800) 780-7905/
937-5150/inn@oceanfrontmagic.com/www.oceanfrontmagic.com

Anastasia Logan, Box 598, Philo, 95455—895-2524/anastasia@saber.net

The Apple Farm, 18501 Greenwod Road, Philo, 95466
—Tel & Fax 895-2461/895-2333

Bay View Cafe, 45040 Main, Mendocino, 95460—937-4197

Blackberry Inn, 44951 Larkin Rd., Mendocino, 95460
—(800) 950-7806/937-5281/blackber@mcn.org

Bluebird Cafe, 13340 South Highway 101, Hopland, 95449
—744-1633/www.mendofood.com

The Blue Victorian Inn & Antique Shop, 38911 Main/North Highway 1,
Box 213, Westport, 95488—(800) 400-6310/964-6310/www.bluevictorian.com

Cafe Beaujolais, 961 Ukiah Street, Box 1236, Mendocino, 95460
—937-5614/Fax 937-3656/www.cafebeaujolais.com

Eagle Rock Gourmet Lamb, Stanley Johnson, 42400 Highway 128, Cloverdale,
95425—894-2814

Elk Cove Inn, 6300 South Highway 1, Box 367, Elk, 95432
—(800) 275-2967/877-3321/elkcove@mcn.org/www.elkcoveinn.com

Etta Place Bed & Breakfast Inn, 909 Exley Lane, Willits, 95490
—459-5953/krkirk@mcn.org/www.lodgingontheweb.com

Fensalden Inn, 33810 Navarro Ridge Road, Box 99, Albion, 95410
—(800) 959-3850/937-4042/Fax 937-2416/www.fensalden.com

Fuller's Fine Herbs, Box 1344, Mendocino, 95460—937-0860/fuller4h@mcn.org

Good Thyme Herb Company, Box 975, Mendocino, 95460
—Tel & Fax 964-0509/goodthym@mcn.org/www.goodthyme.com

Gowan's Oak Tree, 6600 Highway 128, Philo, 95466
—895-3353/895-3225/ cecil@pacific.net

Great Chefs of Mendocino, Box 771, Hopland, 95449—Tel & Fax 468-5538/
syundt@pacific.net/www.mendofod.com

Greenwood Pier Inn & Cafe, 5926 South Highway 1, Box 336, Elk, 95432 —877-9997/www.greenwoodpierinn.com
The Grey Whale Inn, 615 N. Main, Fort Bragg, 95437—(800)-382-7244/ 964-0640/Fax 964-4408/gwhale@mcn.org/www.greywhaleinn.com
Harvest Market, 171 Boatyard Drive, Boatyard Center, Highways 1 & 20, Fort Bragg, 95437—964-7000/www.harvestmarket.com
Herbal Elegance Catering, Box 177, Comptche, 95427—937-1651/liz@mcn.org/ www.herbalelegance.com
Heritage House, 5200 North Highway 1, Little River, 95456—(800) 235-5885/ 937-5141/Fax 937-0318/hh@mcn.org/www.heritagehouseinn.com
The Hill House Inn, 10701 Palette Drive, Mendocino, 95460 —(800) 422-0554/937-0554/Fax 937-1123/www.hilhouseinn.com
In A Jam, Richard Rizzolo, 12200 Pine Ave., Potter Valley, 95469 —743-1365/dccxs@pacific.net
Joshua Grindle Inn, 44800 Little Lake, Box 647, Mendocino, 95460 —(800) 474-6353/937-4143/joshgrin@mcn.org/www.joshgrin.com
The Larkin Cottage, 44950 Larkin Road, Mendocino, 95460 —937-2567/Fax 937-4714/stay@larkincottage.com/www.larkincottage.com
Ledford House, 3000 North Highway 1, Albion, 95410 —937 0282/ledford@ledfordhouse.com/www.ledfordhouse.com
Lipinski's Mendo Juice Joint, Ukiah Street east of Lansing Street, Mendocino, 95460—937-4033
The Lodge at Noyo River, 500 Casa del Noyo Drive, Fort Bragg, 95437 —(800) 628-1126/964-8045/Fax 964-9366/www.mcn.org/a/noyoriver/
The MacCallum House Inn, 45020 Albion Street, Box 206, Mendocino, 95460 —(800) 609-0492/937-0289/machouse@mcn.org/www.maccallumhouse.com
The Melting Pot, Corner Main & Lansing, Mendocino, 95460—937-0173
Mendo Bistro, Upstairs at The Company Store, 301 North Main Street, Fort Bragg, 95437—964-4974/Fax 964-4949/nicholas@mcn.org/www.mendobistro.com
Mendocino Cookie Company, 10450 Lansing, Mendocino, 95460—937-4843 & The Company Store, 303 N. Main, Fort Bragg, 95437—964-0282/ www.mendocinocookies.com
Mendocino Farmers' Market—937-2728
Mendocino Hotel, 45080 Main Street, Mendocino, 95460 —(800) 548-0513/937-0511/Fax 937-0513/www.mendocinohotel.com
Mendocino Mustard, 1260 North Main, Fort Bragg, 95437—(800) 964-2270/964-2250
Mendocino Sea Vegetable Company, Box 1265, Mendocino, 95460 —937-2050/info@seaweed.net/www.seaweed.net
Mendosa's Market, 10501 Lansing, Mendocino, 95460—937-5879
The Mole Ranch—877-3524/poet@mcn.org/www.The-Mole-Ranch.com
Munchies Gourmet To Go, 13275 South Highway 101, #7, Hopland, 95449 —744-1600/www.mendofood.com
North Coast Country Inn, 34591 South Highway 1, Gualala, 95445 —(800) 959-4537/884-4537/mtopping@aol.com/www.northcountryinn.com
The Old Milano Hotel & Restaurant, 38300 South Highway 1, Gualala, 95445 —884-3256/coast@oldmilanohotel.com/www.oldmilanohotel.com

Old Stewart House Inn, 511 Stewart Street, Fort Bragg, 95437—(800) 287-8392/ 961-0775/darrell@oldstewarthouseinn.com/www.mcn.org/d/galli/

Oz Farm Retreat, Box 244, Point Arena, 95468—882-3046/(415) 626-8880/ ozfarm@aol.com/members.aol.com/ozfarms/oz.htm

The Phantom Cafe

The Philo Pottery Inn, 8550 Highway 128, Box 166, Philo, 95466 —895-3069/philoinn@pacific.net/www.innaccess.com/PHI/

The Ravens Restaurant at The Stanford Inn by the Sea, Coast Highway 1 & Comptche-Ukiah Road, Box 487, Mendocino, 95460—(800) 331-8884/937-5615/ Fax 937-0305/www.mcn.org/a/stanfordinn

The Restaurant, 418 North Main, Fort Bragg, 95437—964-9800

Reed Manor, Pallet Drive, Box 127, Mendocino, 95460 —937-5446/mreed@mcn.org/www.reedmanor.com

Scharffen Berger Chocolate Maker, Inc., 250 South Maple Avenue Unit C, South San Francisco, 94080—(800) 930-4528/(650) 866-3300/Fax (650) 866-3301/ bean2bar@scharffen-berger.com/www.scharffen-berger.com/

Sharon Robinson's Wedding Cakes & Wonderful Desserts, Box 1118, Mendocino, 95460—962-0384/sharon@mendocake.com/www.mendocakes.com

St. Orres Restaurant, 36601 Highway 1, Box 523, Gualala, 95445 —884-3303/884-3335/Fax 884-1840/rosemary@mcn.org/www.saintorres.com

Stevenswood Lodge, 8211 North Highway 1, Little River—Box 170, Mendocino, 95460—(800) 421-2810/937-2810/Fax 937-1237/www.stevenswood.com

Thatcher Inn, 13401 South Highway 101, Hopland, 95449 —(800) 266-1891/744-1890/info@thatcherinn.com/www.thatcherinn.com

Tobina's (Tobina's All-Natural Teriyaki), Box 1467, Ukiah, 95482 —462-9269/442-4144/tobine@jpg.net/www.1gourmet.com

Victorian Farmhouse, 7001 North Highway 1, Little River, 95456 —(800) 264-4723/937-0697/Fax 937-5238/frednjo@victorianfarmhouse.com/ www.victorianfarmhouse.com

Victorian Gardens, 14409 South Highway 1, Manchester, 95459—882-3606

Well House West, 311 North Franklin, Fort Bragg, 95437—964-2101

The Weller House Inn, 524 Stewart, Fort Bragg, 95437—(877) 893-5537/ 964-4415/innkeeper@wellerhouse.com/www.wellerhouse.com

Whale Watch Inn by the Sea Bread & Breakfast, 35100 South Highway 1, Gualala, 95445—(800) 942-5342/884-3667/Fax 964-4198/whale@mcn.org/ www.whale-watch.com

Whitegate Inn, 499 Howard, Box 150, Mendocino, 95460—(800) 531-7282/ 937-4892/Fax 937-1131/innkeepers@whitegateinn.com/www.whitegateinn.com

Zack's Catering, 1021 Hops Estate Lane, Ukiah, 95482 —(888) 505-8484/468-8484/575-7211/Fax 468-0395/zack@zackscatering.com/ www.zackscatering.com

Index of Recipes

Index